MONEY
BEFORE
MARRIAGE

*A Financial Workbook
for Engaged Couples*

LARRY
BURKETT

WITH MICHAEL E. TAYLOR

MONEY
BEFORE
MARRIAGE

*A Financial Workbook
for Engaged Couples*

LARRY
BURKETT

WITH MICHAEL E. TAYLOR

MOODY PRESS

CHICAGO

Scripture taken from from the *New American Standard Bible,* © 1960, 1962, 1963, 1968, 1971, 1972, 1973, 1975, 1977 by the Lockman Foundation. Used by permission.

Edited by Adeline Griffith, Christian Financial Concepts.

ISBN: 0-8024-6389-4

7 9 10 8 6

Printed in the United States of America

TABLE OF CONTENTS

Michael Taylor works in the Career Pathways department at Christian Financial Concepts, and is a freelance writer and columnist for various newspapers. He was a pastor and church planter for twenty years.

ACKNOWLEDGEMENT

There are several people I would like to thank for their efforts in completing this pre-marriage workbook.

Lee Ellis and the staff of Career Pathways contributed the personality and financial management surveys, and Peter Pace created the layout and design for the personality survey.

Mike Taylor developed the project while I recuperated from my cancer surgeries, and my editor Adeline Griffith ensured quality text on each page.

Without the help of these people this book would not have been a reality. It's my prayer that God will use this workbook to help establish strong marriages and thereby stem the tide of divorces in our land.

INTRODUCTORY
Notes from Larry

Few events in life tap as deeply into the hopes and aspirations of the human soul as getting married. The announcement of plans to be united as husband and wife is indeed a great joy to be celebrated.

Your wedding provides a unique moment in time for your families, along with your church family, to bless you as you witness to God's leading in your life.

As the Giver of "*every good and perfect gift*," God is to be praised for creating the institution of marriage. And we at Christian Financial Concepts offer our congratulations to you as your wedding plans take shape.

As you well know, with every freedom comes an equal amount of responsibility, and the step of entering the marriage relationship is no exception. Your choice to get married will create responsibilities for the rest of your lives. And so, this weighty decision deserves your full attention and preparation.

After all, who enters the marriage relationship with the intention of getting divorced? Yet, couples who marry for the first time continue to face a 50 percent chance of divorce during their lifetimes according to the National Center for Health Statistics. And for second marriages which involve children, the divorce rate rises to 65 percent.

I believe it is possible for you to get married and remain married. Divorce is not inevitable. That doesn't mean you won't have trials, struggles, and surprise adjustments to make. You will. Every marriage does, but a couple faithfully committed to Jesus Christ will emerge from those trials stronger.

To help prepare you for married life, I have developed this premarital couples' workbook. In addition to the excitement of the wedding plans, announcements, parties, and showers, there are some very practical steps of preparation for life after the ceremony.

By carefully using this workbook, you will be challenged to evaluate key areas that might otherwise be overlooked. Since the workbook cannot cover training in every conceivable problem area of marriage, the chapters are written about the following particular areas.

First, you'll study the application of God's Word to marriage and family. When starting a project, it always helps to read the directions. Marriage is no exception. In the Bible, God offers countless principles to make your marriage incredibly great. Chapter 1 addresses how management of your individual finances can really help you know one another.

A second subject you'll study is learning to communicate in marriage. Chapter 2 will help you and your spouse to discover the strengths and weaknesses of your God-given personalities. In addition, you'll be trained to use communication skills that enhance cooperation and also identify negative patterns that create disruption and isolation.

For the past five years our Career Pathways division has researched the relationship between personality and work success. Their insights will help you to discover how God is weaving your two personalities into an effective team. You will be blessed as you sense the wonder of His providential leading in your lives.

Chapters 3 and 4 will help you discover the practical aspects of managing your personal finances in marriage. You'll be challenged to assess your current financial situation and develop a realistic budget for your first year of marriage. You'll also discover if you're primarily a "spender" or "hoarder" when it comes to handling money. This material may open some good conversations between the two of you.

Teaching God's people the biblical principles of handling money has been on my heart for many years. The principles I offer you come from more than twenty years of personal Bible study, coupled with the experiences of counseling literally hundreds and hundreds of couples in financial trouble. I invite you to learn from the mistakes of others who, incidentally, began their marriages just as enthusiastically as you are.

In Chapter 5, important marriage issues are presented in a question and answer format. If I were able to sit down with you personally for premarital counseling, these are key principles and insights I would give to every couple.

And there's one more thing. I've always said that personal finances are an outward indicator of a person's inward spiritual condition. By carefully using this workbook, you very likely will discover more about one another.

And frankly, you may decide to postpone or call off your marriage. As many as 10 percent of couples going through rigorous premarital counseling programs make that choice. It takes courage. You may suffer profound personal consequences as a result. *But isn't it better to back off prior to marriage than to forge ahead, knowing in your heart that you are making a mistake?*

I encourage you to become accountable to your pastor as you complete this workbook. This material will help you to focus your premarital counseling time with him. To assist in this effort, Chapter 6 has been added to the workbook as a supplement for your pastor. Show this workbook to him.

Your engagement period is the perfect time for you to become settled on a church family. Look for a church where other young couples are involved and growing in the Lord. Christian fellowship brings a wealth of encouragement during this important transition time in your lives.

I realize that the six to nine months prior to a wedding can be chaotic and hectic. It will not be easy for you to carve out time for these in-depth studies. But the truth is, time pressures seldom disappear after marriage. You have to begin "doing the right thing" for your marriage now . . . and resolve to continue elevating your marriage to the highest priority in the years ahead.

God bless you as you pursue your plans for marriage.

A SPECIAL WORD TO NEWLYWEDS

The language in this workbook presupposes that you are still engaged. Nonetheless, since the first few years of marriage require many adjustments, the surveys will be just as helpful for you as newlyweds. In fact, these materials may help you to understand some of the differences you've already discovered in your relationship.

CHAPTER 1

Finances: The Doorway to Intimacy

CHAPTER 1

Finances: The Doorway to Intimacy

"**A**nd we're the perfect couple, Pastor Smith," Susan stated, beaming with pride. "I just love everything about Jeff." Her eyes quickly shifted to Jeff, who sat stoically beside her in the pastor's office.

"I'm sure you do," replied Pastor Smith, "but let's get back to the topic for tonight's session: conflict resolution. Why don't you describe for me how you settle your disagreements? Maybe you can think of a recent example."

"Oh, we never fuss with one another," Susan replied. "We've been engaged for six months now and never have had an argument. Isn't that wonderful? See how perfectly matched we are for one another?" Once again her eyes shot a quick glance toward Jeff, searching for his approval. Jeff silently nodded in agreement.

With his thick eyebrows raised, Pastor Smith drew a deep breath and continued. "Well, Susan, that concerns me. Part of being prepared for marriage is really getting to know one another's strengths and weaknesses. And one of the goals of your engagement is to focus on being able to communicate with one another because, after marriage, every couple will have conflicts to resolve. So good communication is vital to a happy marriage."

"What about you, Jeff?" probed Pastor Smith. "Can you think of a time when you disagreed with Susan, and how you worked out your differences?"

At the sound of his name, Jeff roused to attention. "Uh . . . I agree with what Susan said. We never disagree."

Susan eased back from the edge of her seat, relaxing against the back of the chair, feeling quite comfortable indeed. "See, I told you, Pastor. We're a perfect match for one another."

Who doesn't enter marriage feeling like the "perfect couple"? Everyone should! In fact, if you're not convinced that the two of you have a unique relationship, you should reconsider getting married until you are convinced.

While growing in a dating relationship, most people put their "best foot forward." You probably have too. After all, you're doing your best to attract your future lifelong mate. But as the relationship grows more and more intimate, it reaches a critical turning point: Your shortcomings become apparent; you can't hide them any longer. You "let your hair down," you relax more in the relationship, and pretense falls away. This stage is predictable and essential.

Good marriages are not the result of some mysterious "ideal" combination of personality matches. No one is perfect, and every marriage requires challenging adjustments. Good marriages don't just happen; they are made by two people who are committed to one another for better or for worse, period. (A frustrated wife once complained, "Yeah, but he's worse than I took him for!")

Becoming acquainted with both strengths and weaknesses is a critical part of relationships. Not liking what they see, many break off the engagement. That's wise. It's better to courageously face this painful choice before marriage than live to with the consequences afterward.

But incredibly, other couples postpone this step and jeopardize the foundation of their marriage. Then, when conflicts occur, they figure they just weren't matched to the right spouse in the first place. As a result, nearly one in every two couples vowing "till death do us part" gets divorced. Why? How can so many people who are so in love, who launched into marital bliss with such promise, be so mistaken?

And the real question is, what can you do prior to marriage to be as prepared as possible? Part of the answer is really getting to know one another and the core values you bring to the marriage.

Money Management Reveals the Real You

How people manage their personal finances can actually function like a doorway to intimacy, helping them to really know one another. When it comes to impressing others, people can say anything they think others want to hear. Many are great at faking their true attitudes. The way they handle their finances, however, is usually a dead giveaway to what is really going on. That's because managing money reveals the spiritual issues and values of their lives.

What's true for others is true for the two of you as well. By being candid about your attitudes and methods of money management, you can discover some of the following core values and attitudes that the two of you have.

- selfishness versus cooperation
- pride versus humility
- self-control versus impulsiveness
- trusting God versus rebellion or independence
- greed versus generosity

- sacrifice versus immediate self-gratification
- your patterns of decision making
- your patterns for disagreement
- priority of eternal versus earthly values
- planning versus being disorganized

Watch for God to use money in your marriage to illustrate the following biblical truths.

1. **God uses money to demonstrate His faithfulness.** Just prior to Israel's entrance into the Promised Land, Moses reminded the people that it was God who would give them the power to make wealth (Deuteronomy 8:11–18). Money is one way that God reveals His faithfulness. Your security is in God, not in your bank account. Discovering His faithfulness through your financial needs encourages your reliance on Him in every area of life. Be careful, however, not to confuse your needs and your wants.

2. **God uses money to stimulate your prayer life.** In Matthew 7:7–8, Jesus teaches three intensity levels of prayer: asking, seeking, and knocking. Some financial matters will be resolved simply by **asking** God. Others will require **seeking** in prayer, an activity that requires your investment of time and effort. Finally, to gain some answers, **knocking** in prayer is required. This deeper level of prayer requires not only your time and energy but persistence and repetition. Financial stress can deepen your prayer life.

3. **God uses money to reveal your need of the Savior.** The management of money potentially can provoke sinful attitudes and behaviors in marriage, similar to swatting a hornet's nest. The apostle Paul teaches that *"those who are in the flesh cannot please God"* (Romans 8:8). No one is perfect. God uses money to demonstrate your daily need for the Savior, Jesus Christ.

4. **God uses money to cultivate self-control.** Listed among the fruits of the Spirit in Galatians 5, self-control is a key aspect of successful money management. The inability to stop spending in America's materialistic culture is a prescription for trouble. *"Like a city that is broken into and without walls is a man who has no control over his spirit"* (Proverbs 25:28).

5. **God uses money to clarify your life values.** Many worldly temptations will clamor for your attention. I believe you can tell a great deal about your spiritual maturity by how you spend your money. Managing money requires that you clarify your life values, set priorities, and make choices, thus serving as a self-test in the faith (see 2 Corinthians 13:5). Jesus said, *"But seek first His kingdom and His righteousness; and all these things shall be added to you"* (Matthew 6:33).

6. **God uses money to teach cooperation in marriage.** Both of you already have deeply embedded financial values, goals, and dreams. It's not unusual for these competing agendas to spark division, especially early in marriage. God has a better plan. His desire is that money management will forge cooperation in your marriage, not only to your benefit, but as a witness to those who are not yet saved. *"Be subject to one another in the fear of Christ"* (Ephesians 5:21). Cooperating necessarily involves yielding your personal rights in favor of what's best for the marriage, as seen in the following testimony.

THE VOICE OF EXPERIENCE—from John and Annette, Mitchellville, Maryland, married 4/3/93

"No more his money, her money, but our money. You can accomplish more in harmony than you ever can with everything separate. Following this advice has benefited us many times over. It wasn't easy to discuss and set up the budget, agree upon financial goals and trust each other with access to all the accounts. But we have done it and we have learned to rely upon each other."

Regardless of who makes the most money, it is essential that you operate in the "our money" frame of mind—not "my money" or "her money" or "his money." There are choices about money to be made nearly every day. When you are married, those choices need to be made together because this is a joint venture, not two corporations doing business under one roof!

This is not an easy adjustment to make since you have been accustomed to making decisions about money on your own and probably feel you are pretty good at it. You must now consider the feelings and thoughts of your "other half" as you make these decisions. This could be difficult unless you make the effort to communicate well.

To promote the best communication and teamwork skills, I encourage both of you to spend time together each month reviewing your budget. Don't let the responsibility for your finances fall on just one person. Instead, discuss your spending habits and the outstanding bills you have to pay. Pray about your needs and ask God to lead you in setting goals that both of you agree on. Resolve to let money management forge a deeper unity in your marriage rather than drive a wedge between you.

Although both of you should know how to balance your bank statement, pay the bills, and handle all the details, I suggest that only one person keep the books. You can rotate these responsibilities every six months or so, but two people cannot simultaneously keep the records. Don't try.

Instead, get into the habit of discussing finances each month as you pay the bills and work the budget. Once you reach an agreement, only one person is needed to actually write the checks and handle the paperwork. Keep in mind that the relationship is worth far more than any budget item under discussion.

Toward a Biblical Attitude on Finances

Virtually everything done today has a cost factor to it, which makes it essential to get your attitudes about money straight to begin with. Jesus said, *"Where your treasure is, there will your heart be also"* (Matthew 6:21). You may enjoy all the things you are allowed to have, but you must never allow them to become the object of worship. Your real treasure is not here in this world anyway. Rather, it is in the world that is to come.

Why do you think your attitude about money is important to God? _____

_____

_____

There is a difference between resources or wealth provided by God and those things provided by the world. *"It is the blessing of the Lord that makes rich, and He adds no sorrow to it"* (Proverbs 10:22). This is how you can tell if the blessing is from the Lord or not: Does it bring sorrow? Are the payments more than you can afford, or do they cause arguments between you?

One thing you can know is that God is not going to send something into your lives to cause you to become so embittered that you can't stand each other. If you are facing a decision, ask yourselves: Will the decision bring peace or strife? A decision made only on the financial merits often is the wrong one. Jesus said, *"No one can serve two masters . . . . You cannot serve God and mammon"* (Matthew 6:24).

How can your decisions reflect whether you are choosing God or money first?

_____

_____

Everything actually belongs to the Lord. Psalm 24:1 says, *"The earth is the Lord's, and all it contains."* The fact is, you actually don't own anything in the long-term sense; you are just **managers**. You know that you can't take anything with you at death; you don't see U-Haul trailers being pulled by hearses on the way to the cemetery! The difficulty is remembering your position as managers, while you are here and acting from that position, rather than thinking you "own" things.

X   How can you reinforce with one another this attitude of being managers rather than owners? _____

_____

_____

Can you think of any advantages to being a manager of things rather than an owner? Scripture seems to indicate that there is a great advantage. Jesus said, *"He who is faithful in a very little thing is faithful also in much"* (Luke 16:10). If you learn to be faithful with what you have in the early years of your marriage, the Lord will entrust you with more to manage as you demonstrate the ability to be faithful.

Does this mean that if you really try to be good managers God is obligated to give you more? _____ yes _____ no

Is there a penalty for not being a good manager? Aside from the obvious fact that you will have less to show for it later, there is also the example given in Matthew 25:14–30, in which the unfaithful manager was stripped of all responsibilities and thrown out "into the outer darkness." You may not be sure exactly where that person was sent, but you don't want to find out firsthand either!

What important principles do you think this story reveals about God's perspective on our personal money management? _____

_____

_____

If the resources don't actually **belong** to us, why do so many people struggle so hard to gain more? Jesus said, *"Beware, and be on your guard against every form of greed; for not even when one has an abundance does his life consist of his possessions"* (Luke 12:15). There is a belief today that somewhere out there is a level of abundance that will guarantee happiness and protect you against all the trials of life. This is one of Satan's best lies.

In truth, money does not bring happiness. In fact, it can divert your attention enough that you won't realize what has been taken away from you (peace of mind) until it is too late. There is real treasure and contentment in having enough—but none in being a slave to it.

Another factor that can cause you to overextend yourselves is that of greed or envy. Comparison between your situation and someone else's is destructive, leading to resentment and bitterness. According to the Scriptures, you are to be content with what you have (Hebrews 13:5). This is not an easy attitude to cultivate because of a natural desire to have more and more material things.

Ad agencies make it easy to believe that if you don't have all the nice things you see advertised, you just aren't worthy! That's just another one of Satan's lies. In God's eyes, everyone has worth. You are worth the blood of His Son!

X How can you balance your attempts to improve your situation and still learn to be content with what you have? _____
_____
_____

As I mentioned earlier, how you handle your money is an indicator of your inward spiritual condition and, to an extent, it reflects the strength of your relationship.

If the two of you are saved and committed Christians and are working hard at a good relationship, your finances will reflect this fact. This is not a guarantee that you will be rich but, far more important, you will have peace about what you do have. The lack of material things will not be a source of strife in your marriage. You also should remember that your parents took a long time to accumulate the things they have.

X What things do you consider "necessary" to have in the first three years of marriage? _____
_____
_____

One of the most misquoted Scriptures in the Bible is 1 Timothy 6:10: *"For the love of money is a root of all sorts of evil."* When money begins to be the driving force in all you do, you are dangerously close to the condition Paul was talking about here.

One key to avoiding this is to remember that relationships are most important in the long term. Money is not as important as your attitude toward money. If your relationship begins to suffer because of money decisions, examine your attitude.

How can anyone live in a materialistic society like this one and not love money? _____
_____
_____

An important foundation for the marriage you will build is honesty. You can't be honest with God if you aren't honest with each other. In the financial area, complete disclosure of all debts and obligations is essential so there is no misunderstanding later on. An example might be existing child support or alimony payments.

Have you been honest with each other regarding existing debts?

_____ yes _____ no

THE VOICE OF EXPERIENCE— from Kevin and Karen, Richland, Washington, married 8/14/93

"Neither of us had debt of any sort when we became husband and wife. That in and of itself was a real blessing due to the two very unexpected things that happened in our first year of marriage.

"First, we were pleased and surprised to discover we were going to be parents. Second, three months into my term, Kevin was diagnosed with Hodgkins' disease—(cancer of the lymph nodes). Talk about an emotional roller coaster! We were thrilled at the reality of having a baby, yet devastated at the doctor's report for Kevin . . . we continued to tithe at least 10 percent of our income . . . .

"If we had not been 'avid savers' along with not having any debt (we have two great, older used Plymouths that we paid cash for), who knows how we would have paid for those doctor bills . . . .

"Oh, Kevin has been in remission since October, '94 and four days after our one year anniversary, our beautiful baby daughter was born. Unfortunately, our daughter has a small hole in a heart valve. We are praying for it to close on its own, but if it doesn't, she'll need an expensive surgery to close it when she is two years old (August, '96).

"Please remind your readers that a 'rainy day/emergency' fund is not a joke. It could save a lot of heartache should the need arise. God provided every penny through our willingness to abide by biblical financial principles."

CHAPTER 2

Discovering Your Personality Profiles

CHAPTER 2

Discovering Your Personality Profiles

"I'm sick and tired of you cutting me down all the time," fumed Jeff. And with that he slammed the carport door. Susan's eyes filled with tears as she heard the truck roar to life and abruptly screech from their driveway.

What is going on? Susan thought to herself. *What happened to the Jeff I knew before our marriage?*

As she tried to sort it all out, her sobs momentarily subsided and her thoughts turned to good memories of dating Jeff. He was always such fun. He was light-hearted and witty. His enthusiasm and humor made him the life of any party, and she admired so much about him.

She remembered how he had showered her with affection. Of course, Jeff never did anything halfway. With him, it was all or nothing, feast or famine. He was a master of creating good impressions. On more than one occasion he'd had a dozen roses delivered to her office, making her feel like a queen and inciting the envy of her coworkers. The memories caused her eyes to blur with tears again, but she quickly wiped them away with the back of her hand.

Now, after nearly a year of marriage, Susan sat alone at her kitchen table, quite bewildered by it all. Jeff seemed to be a different man. He seemed so disorganized and impulsive now, living day to day without a plan. He didn't know what a list was, much less know how to use one.

She had hoped they would slow down—indeed, settle down—after marriage. But like a butterfly, Jeff's attention seemed to flit from one thing to another. She never knew what to expect, leaving her uncertain and insecure.

Deep inside, fear began to gnaw in her stomach. What would things be like in another year? This was not what she had hoped for from marriage. Unable to fight back the tears again, Susan buried her face in her trembling arms and sobbed uncontrollably.

Jeff rammed the stick into fourth gear as his customized truck darted down the freeway ramp. *What gives with Susan, anyway?* he muttered under his breath. *If I say black, she says white. I'm getting a bellyful of her criticizing everything I do,* he thought.

He jerked his left blinker on, accelerated into an open slot in traffic, and raced down the Santa Monica freeway, radio blaring all the way.

While they were dating, Susan was always so supportive. She loved his ideas, and his self-confidence swelled in light of her respect. She was quite content to follow his lead.

And Jeff was equally attracted to Susan. She had a list for everything. When they planned outings together, she would whip out her purse calendar, on which she had the next two months scheduled. Now her calendar had become a straitjacket for him. Susan didn't want to do anything if it wasn't "on the calendar."

Once Jeff had been genuinely amused by Susan as they checked out in a grocery store. Calculator in hand, she kept a running total of all her purchases, thus beating the checkout clerk to the total due. She was seldom wrong.

As the novelty of married life wore off, however, it just seemed like Susan became more and more stubborn. And picky: pick up your clothes; quit squeezing the toothpaste from the middle and put the cap back on; wash the car; replace the toilet paper over the top, not from underneath. Her nagging voice droned on and on.

Nothing he could do suited her, and it seemed the harder he tried, the more she cautiously second-guessed him, leaving him completely exasperated. *What happened to the girl I married?*

Perhaps you've heard the saying: Before marriage, opposites *attract;* afterward, they *attack*. It appears that Jeff and Susan are experiencing some of that dynamic in their marriage. In all probability, neither has changed much. However, each person's *perception* of the other has changed.

Carefully study the diagram below to discern both an elderly woman and a beautiful young woman.

The picture illustrates the fact that *we're able to look at the same situation and see things differently.* Jeff and Susan both had weaknesses associated with their personalities all along. Earlier, the intensity of courtship and romance caused the two to accentuate the positive, attractive elements of their personalities, while camouflaging their weaknesses. But after settling into their marriage relationship, these weaknesses became more evident. Consider the testimony on the next page.

THE VOICE OF EXPERIENCE— from **Kelly and Holly, Monroe, Washington,** married 11/93.

"I thought it was funny that so many of the stereotypes about men and women were so true. The remote control was amazing to me. My husband would click through thirty channels in a couple of minutes and say, 'There's nothing on.' I'm like, 'How can you possibly tell? You only saw each channel for a couple of seconds and half of them were on commercials!' And all of that with the TV Guide two feet away! And men really do watch two or three shows at once. One night I brought work home and was working at the table. My husband was watching TV and I was half listening as I worked. After about an hour I just had to stop and see what was going on. I couldn't figure out why all the cops were doing kung fu and what all that had to do with elephants!"

Being Opposites Can Be a Positive

In His wisdom, God made opposites to attract. Being attracted to opposite qualities in each other can have many benefits. Imagine how awkward it would be if both of you had a bad sense of direction; but, if one of you has this quality, at least you will know where you are.

This way one of you always knows where you are. Of course, the other usually insists that he or she knows, but I can attest to the fact that usually that person is wrong.

Having opposite personality characteristics can be an asset in handling money as well. One person will have a bent toward budgeting and saving; the other will lean toward spending and borrowing. The amount of leaning in either direction will depend on individual personality.

Included in this workbook is a simple survey to help you determine what your money management tendencies are. Because of your particular blend of personalities, however, it is likely that one of you will be better at keeping the books, and the other can set goals and make decisions more easily.

You also may find that God created you both with very similar personality characteristics. Through your **combined** strengths, you may discover that God will enable your marriage to become a unique blessing to others.

However, whether you are alike or different, marriage presents every couple with the challenge of working together. Therefore, it is important to decide before getting married if both of you are willing to set aside your individual rights and work as one. If not, then stop and seriously reconsider getting married. As difficult as it might seem to break an engagement, let me assure you that to break up a marriage is a thousand times more grievous. Unfortunately, in our society today it is all too common.

Biblical Communication Principles That Work

Since God is the one who designed you and your spouse with particular personality characteristics, He also has given you His wisdom for how to live with one another and enjoy it. The Bible is the "operator's manual" for marriage, and if you ignore it you will miss a lot of valuable information.

I've listed below five biblical principles that will enrich your marriage. If you faithfully practice them, you will minimize Satan's opportunities to drive a wedge in your relationship.

1. Speak the truth; don't make excuses or tell lies. A good marriage is built on a foundation of trust. It doesn't take many lies to destroy that foundation (Ephesians 4:25).

2. Don't keep things bottled up until you explode. Settle differences before you go to bed; it doesn't get easier to resolve difficulties with time, it gets harder. Satan has a chance to give you more arguments to throw at your partner, and your position becomes more firm—until you're "set in concrete." Discuss your differences as early as you can while the issue is still fresh (Ephesians 4:26–27).

3. Learn to work on the problem, not the person. Step back into the third-party position and seek a solution other than punishing the one who created the problem. It's a more appropriate and productive action since you are neither God nor that person's parent. It also takes off some of the pressure (Ecclesiastes 4:9–12).

4. At every opportunity, repay evil with good. Study how Joseph responded to the ill will of his brothers in Genesis 50:19–20. Then read the example of Jesus cited in 1 Peter 2:23. Frequently the person who seems to have his or her mind made up on an issue will respond to grace and a tender word (see Ephesians 4:31–32).

5. Model the love of Christ to one another. God intends for the two of you to practice, model, and demonstrate to unbelievers what His love, grace, and forgiveness are like. To be sure, two people with different personalities will have misunderstandings and, as a result, disagreements. By understanding how personality tendencies influence your behavior, such as why you approach a problem a certain way, you may be able to anticipate the difficulty before it occurs and avoid it. Not only is that good for your marriage, it's a positive witness of God's presence in your relationship (1 Peter 2:11–12; Ephesians 5:22–23)

The Couples Communication Survey contained in this chapter will help the two of you to discover the strengths and weaknesses associated with your personality. Knowing this information *prior* to marriage will enable you to sharpen your communication skills and minimize surprise adjustments and disappointments after your marriage.

It's important to note that the survey is not a test to determine whether you should marry. There are no "best" combinations of personalities that create an ideal marriage. What is most important in maximizing your marriage relationship is for each of you to live under the Lordship of Jesus Christ. In that sense, the best temperament is a Spirit-filled temperament.

The purpose of the Communications Survey is to help you identify your strengths and weaknesses and to improve your communication styles in light of them.

CAREER PATHWAYS

Couples
Communication
Survey

BEGIN HERE

↓

INTRODUCTION TO THE COUPLES COMMUNICATION SURVEY

This self-scoring assessment tool will help you and your future spouse to discover more about your natural, God-given temperaments and personalities. By learning more about your motivations, you will be better equipped to understand yourself and one another.

This survey booklet contains two personality surveys, one for each person. For simplicity, the first survey is marked for the husband and the second for the wife. Because the surveys are not tests, there are no right or wrong answers. Neither are the surveys a "test" to determine if you should marry. There is no "right or wrong" matchup of personality patterns. The goal is to simply identify your natural behavior and that of your spouse and to learn how to maximize your communication.

BEFORE YOU TAKE THE SURVEY, READ THESE CAUTIONS!

1. Personality surveys tend to be influenced by the situational focus a person has when responding. Focus on your natural behavior at home. Remember, this is not a survey of how your future spouse wants you to act but, instead, it is a reflection of your core behavior.

2. Do not look ahead or try to analyze the survey, and do not make assumptions about where it is leading as you are responding. Just follow the instructions, step by step.

3. This survey may look similar to others you have taken, but there are some important differences in the rating system. Be sure you understand the directions and examples.

4. This booklet has been designed to be used by people with varying backgrounds of education and experience. If you will CAREFULLY FOLLOW ALL THE DIRECTIONS AND HEED THE CAUTIONS, you will be able to identify and understand your personality strengths and those of your spouse.

5. Some sections will require you to work together; other sections require individual work. Read the directions carefully.

6. If you are not sure what a word on the survey means, turn to the Appendix on page 117, where you will find DISC Word Definitions.

→

2

Survey A
Husband's Survey

DIRECTIONS

FOCUS: The focus for this survey is **your typical behavior.** Respond based on **how you most naturally behave.**

RESPOND: Rate each line of words from left to right on a 4, 3, 2, 1 scale with <u>4 being the word that best describes your naturally motivated behavior and 1 being the word that is least like you.</u> <u>*Use all ratings (4, 3, 2, 1) in each line and use each rating only once.*</u> To change a response, mark through it and write the new response to the left of the box. Study the example below before starting.

Correct Example A: → [4] Enthusiastic [1] Loyal [2] Detailed [3] Commanding

Incorrect Example B: → [4] Enthusiastic [1] Loyal [3] Detailed [4] Commanding

Incorrect: Use each rating only once as in Example A.

CAUTION: We all have ideas about how we would like to act in order to be more acceptable to others. However, that is not what we are looking for in this survey. Think of your core self, and answer based on your instinctive behavior, regardless of whether you consider it to be good or bad.

4 is most like you ← 4 3 2 1 → 1 is least like you

☐ Enthusiastic	☐ Loyal	☐ Detailed	☐ Commanding
☐ Lenient	☐ Expressive	☐ Decisive	☐ Particular
☐ Convincing	☐ Tough-Minded	☐ Meticulous	☐ Kind
☐ Independent	☐ Follow Rules	☐ Peaceful	☐ Fun-Loving
☐ High Standards	☐ Understanding	☐ People-Oriented	☐ Daring
☐ Charitable	☐ Lively	☐ Risk Taker	☐ Serious
☐ Cheerful	☐ Courageous	☐ Precise	☐ Merciful
☐ Confident	☐ Logical	☐ Supportive	☐ Inspiring
☐ Conscientious	☐ Patient	☐ Good Mixer	☐ Fearless
☐ Non-Conforming	☐ Talkative	☐ Gentle	☐ Analytical
☐ Organized	☐ Assertive	☐ Popular	☐ Even-Paced
☐ Good Listener	☐ Factual	☐ Take-Charge	☐ Uninhibited
☐ Aggressive	☐ Cooperative	☐ Vibrant	☐ Accurate
☐ Efficient	☐ Direct	☐ Gracious	☐ Excitable
☐ Influencing	☐ Accommodating	☐ Focused	☐ Frank
☐ Agreeable	☐ Animated	☐ Forceful	☐ Systematic

When you have completed this survey, turn to page 7 for the wife's survey. →

Survey A
Scoring Key

SCORING YOUR RESULTS

Your responses from the survey have been recorded on this page. Follow the steps below to score your results.

1. Your answers are in boxes labeled D, I, S, or C. Begin with the left column and add all the numbers in the boxes labeled "D" in each column so that you end up with a "D" total for the entire survey. Enter this total on the line labeled "D" at right.

2. Follow the same procedure for boxes labeled I, S, and C, and enter the totals on the appropriate line at right.

3. To check for accuracy, add the totals at right for D, I, S, and C. The check total should be 160. If your check total is different, you either made an error in addition, or you may have used the same number twice on one line of the survey.

4. Finally, transfer your D, I, S, and C totals to the Survey A section at the top of page 11.

Scoring Summary

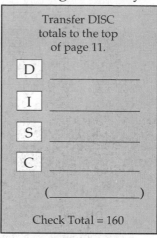

Transfer DISC totals to the top of page 11.

D _____

I _____

S _____

C _____

(_____)

Check Total = 160

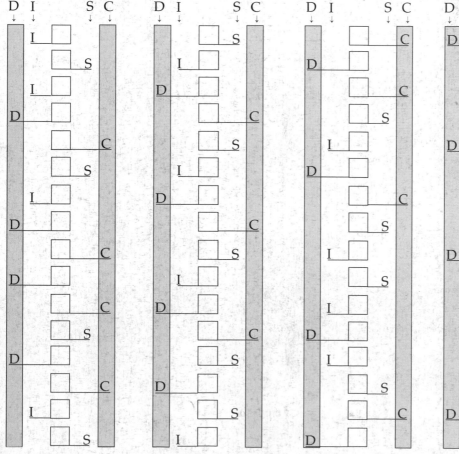

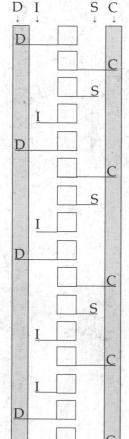

Survey B
Wife's Survey

> **➤ DIRECTIONS**
>
> **FOCUS:** The focus for this survey is **your typical behavior.** Respond based on **how you most naturally behave.**
>
> **RESPOND:** Rate each line of words from left to right on a 4, 3, 2, 1 scale with **4 being the word that best describes your naturally motivated behavior and 1 being the word that is least like you.** *Use all ratings (4, 3, 2, 1) in each line and use each rating only once.* To change a response, mark through it and write the new response to the left of the box. Study the example below before starting.
>
> **Correct** Example A: → `4` Enthusiastic `1` Loyal `2` Detailed `3` Commanding
>
> **Incorrect** Example B: → `4` Enthusiastic `1` Loyal `3` Detailed `4` Commanding
>
>   *Incorrect: Use each rating only once as in Example A.*

CAUTION: We all have ideas about how we would like to act in order to be more acceptable to others. However, that is not what we are looking for in this survey. Think of your core self, and answer based on your instinctive behavior, regardless of whether you consider it to be good or bad.

4 is most like you   ←   4   3   2   1   →   **1 is least like you**

Enthusiastic	Loyal	Detailed	Commanding
Lenient	Expressive	Decisive	Particular
Convincing	Tough-Minded	Meticulous	Kind
Independent	Follow Rules	Peaceful	Fun-Loving
High Standards	Understanding	People-Oriented	Daring
Charitable	Lively	Risk Taker	Serious
Cheerful	Courageous	Precise	Merciful
Confident	Logical	Supportive	Inspiring
Conscientious	Patient	Good Mixer	Fearless
Non-Conforming	Talkative	Gentle	Analytical
Organized	Assertive	Popular	Even-Paced
Good Listener	Factual	Take-Charge	Uninhibited
Aggressive	Cooperative	Vibrant	Accurate
Efficient	Direct	Gracious	Excitable
Influencing	Accommodating	Focused	Frank
Agreeable	Animated	Forceful	Systematic

When you have completed this survey, turn to page 9 and continue.

Survey B
Scoring Key

SCORING YOUR RESULTS

Your responses from the survey have been recorded on this page. Follow the steps below to score your results.

1. Your answers are in boxes labeled D, I, S, or C. Begin with the left column and add all the numbers in the boxes labeled "D" in each column so that you end up with a "D" total for the entire survey. Enter this total on the line labeled "D" at right.

2. Follow the same procedure for boxes labeled I, S, and C, and enter the totals on the appropriate line at right.

3. To check for accuracy, add the totals at right for D, I, S, and C. The check total should be 160. If your check total is different, you either made an error in addition, or you may have used the same number twice on one line of the survey.

4. Finally, transfer your D, I, S, and C totals to the Survey B section at the top of page 11.

Scoring Summary

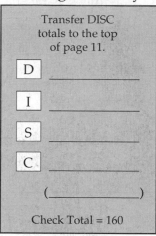

Transfer DISC totals to the top of page 11.

D _____

I _____

S _____

C _____

(_____)

Check Total = 160

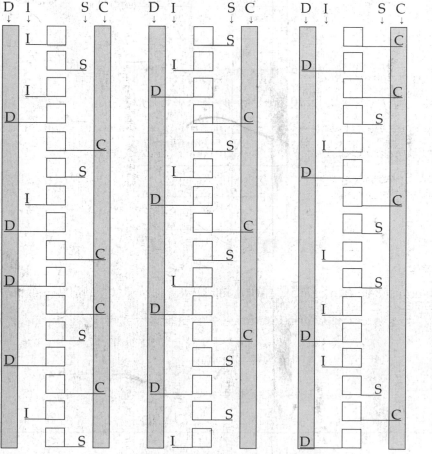

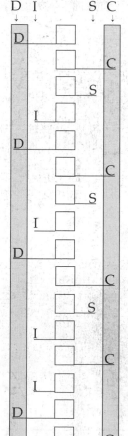

1 Score Your Survey

a. Carefully separate the glued edges that attach pages 3 and 5. Then separate pages 7 and 9.

b. Follow the instructions on the exposed pages and score Survey A and Survey B.

c. Transfer your totals from Survey A and Survey B to the spaces at the top of page 11. You will use these numbers to plot your profiles.

2 Review the Example

a. Look over this example graph below to gain a general idea of what you will be doing next.

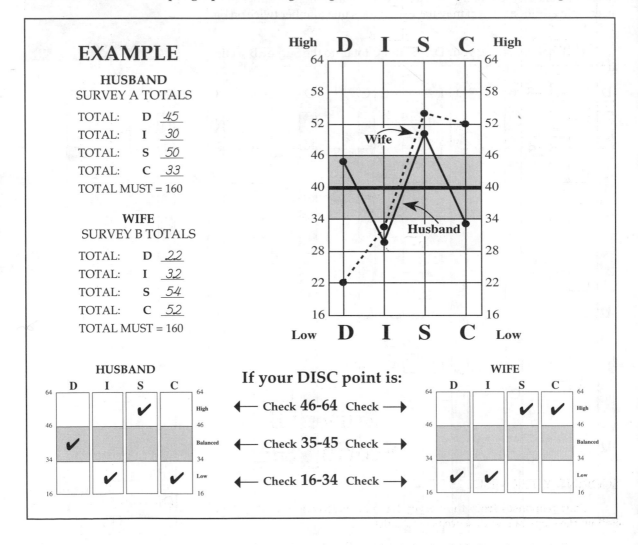

EXAMPLE

HUSBAND
SURVEY A TOTALS

TOTAL: D   _45_
TOTAL: I   _30_
TOTAL: S   _50_
TOTAL: C   _33_
TOTAL MUST = 160

WIFE
SURVEY B TOTALS

TOTAL: D   _22_
TOTAL: I   _32_
TOTAL: S   _54_
TOTAL: C   _52_
TOTAL MUST = 160

If your DISC point is:

← Check **46-64** Check →

← Check **35-45** Check →

← Check **16-34** Check →

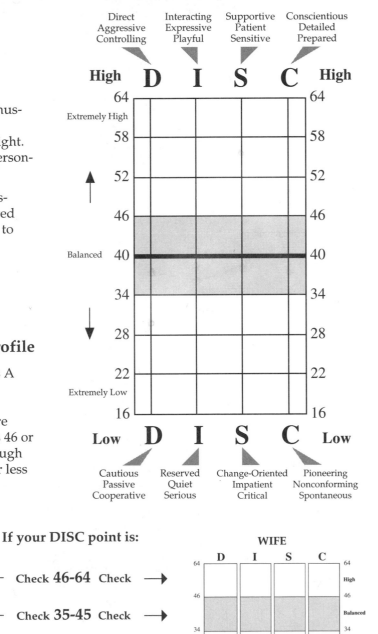

HUSBAND			WIFE		
SURVEY A TOTALS			**SURVEY B TOTALS**		
From page 5			From page 9		
TOTAL:	D	___	TOTAL:	D	___
TOTAL:	I	___	TOTAL:	I	___
TOTAL:	S	___	TOTAL:	S	___
TOTAL:	C	___	TOTAL:	C	___

Direct Aggressive Controlling · Interacting Expressive Playful · Supportive Patient Sensitive · Conscientious Detailed Prepared

High D I S C **High**

3 **Plot Your Profiles**

a. Using the totals from Survey A (husband) & B (wife), plot your DISC dimensions on the graph to the right. The result will be your natural personality profiles.

b. Use a solid line for Survey A (husband) and a dashed line (or colored pencil) for Survey B (wife). Refer to the example on page 10.

64 — Extremely High — 64
58 — 58
52 — 52
46 — 46
40 — Balanced — 40
34 — 34
28 — 28
22 — 22
16 — Extremely Low — 16

4 **Identify Your Natural Profile**

Using your totals from Surveys A (husband) and B (wife), check the appropriate box below to indicate whether your D, I, S, and C points are High, Balanced, or Low. If a point is 46 or more, consider it high. If it is 35 through 45, consider it balanced. Points 34 or less are considered low.

Low D I S C **Low**

Cautious Passive Cooperative · Reserved Quiet Serious · Change-Oriented Impatient Critical · Pioneering Nonconforming Spontaneous

HUSBAND

D I S C
64 / 64 — High
46 / 46 — Balanced
34 / 34 — Low
16 / 16

If your DISC point is:

← Check **46-64** Check →

← Check **35-45** Check →

← Check **16-34** Check →

WIFE

D I S C
64 / 64 — High
46 / 46 — Balanced
34 / 34 — Low
16 / 16

Turn the page and continue. ➡

UNDERSTANDING THE DISC CONCEPT
OF PERSONALITY

INTRODUCTION: This personality discovery instrument is based on the DISC model of personality. DISC comes from the following acrostic, which represents the four primary dimensions of behavior:

D	=	**Dominant**
I	=	**Influencing**
S	=	**Steady**
C	=	**Conscientious**

There are a number of personality surveys that use this four-dimensional DISC system.

In addition, several personality surveys use different terms for these same four dimensions. For instance, Dr. Tim LaHaye and Florence Littauer have written excellent books on temperament using the traditional terminology for these dimensions: Choleric (D), Sanguine (I), Phlegmatic (S), and Melancholy (C). Noted authors, Gary Smalley and John Trent, use the terms Lion (D), Otter (I), Golden Retriever (S), and Beaver (C) in some of their books and presentations to describe these four dimensions.

In order to use the information in this survey, there are several key concepts to understand.

a. We are all born with certain differences in personality and thus are motivated by different circumstances, opportunities, and environments.

b. God has designed us with these differences in motivation in order to serve various functions.

c. Different does not mean wrong; therefore, we should accept and respect those whose personalities are not like ours. It is not our role to change others from the way God made them.

d. All profiles/people have strengths and weaknesses. Profiles should not be used as excuses to ignore bad habits or character flaws.

e. By understanding our personalities, as well as how others are different, we are equipped to better manage our own lives and live more effectively with others.

Review the general characteristics of D, I, S, and C that follow.

➡

The Four Dimensions of DISC

D

DOMINANT: People who have a high level of dominance (High D) are naturally motivated to control the home environment. They are usually assertive, direct, and strong willed. They are typically bold and not afraid to take strong action to get the desired results. They function best in a challenging environment.

Examples:

Joshua	General George Patton
Sarah	Bill Cosby
Solomon	Barbara Walters
Paul	Sam Donaldson

I

INFLUENCING: People who are highly influencing (High I) are driven naturally to relate to others. Usually they are verbal, friendly, outgoing, and optimistic. They are typically enthusiastic motivators and will seek out others to help them accomplish results. They function best in a friendly environment.

Examples:

Peter	President Ronald Reagan
Rebekah	Kathie Lee Gifford
Abigail	John Madden
Barnabas	Joan Rivers

C

CONSCIENTIOUS: People who have a high level of conscientiousness (High C, also called cautiousness) are focused on doing things right. Usually they are detail oriented and find it easy to follow prescribed guidelines. Typically they strive for accuracy and quality and, therefore, set high standards for themselves and for others. They function best in a structured environment.

Examples:

Moses	President Jimmy Carter
Elijah	Albert Einstein
Mary	General Omar Bradley
Luke	David Brinkley

S

STEADY: People who have a high level of steadiness (High S) are naturally motivated to cooperate with and support others. They are usually patient, consistent, and very dependable. Being pleasant and easygoing makes them excellent team players. They function best in a supportive, harmonious environment.

Examples:

Abraham	Pres./Gen. Dwight Eisenhower
Nehemiah	Coach Tom Landry
Hannah	Perry Como
Martha	Mother Teresa

Turn the page and continue.

THIS SAMPLE PAGE will show you how to complete the next four pages which outline the typical strengths and weaknesses of DISC personalities. Based on your Natural Profile from 4 , indicate whether your DISC points are "High," "Balanced," or "Low."

INSTRUCTIONS: Mark the boxes in the left hand margin. **Step #1.** Husbands will check the appropriate box in the "H" column, and wives will use the "W" column. **Step #2.** Now mark the strengths and weaknesses in the appropriate box that describes you.

The example below is taken from the sample graph on page 10. The husband is a "Balanced D" and the wife is a "Low D." They each have marked the strengths and weaknesses that applied to them.

DOMINANT

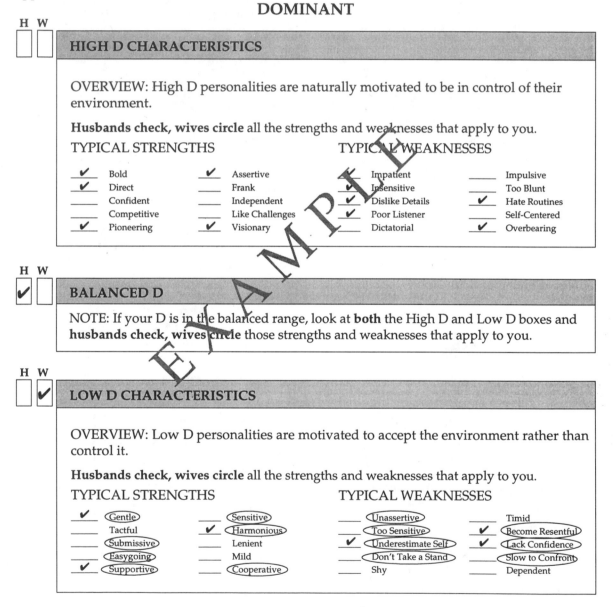

H W

HIGH D CHARACTERISTICS

OVERVIEW: High D personalities are naturally motivated to be in control of their environment.

Husbands check, wives circle all the strengths and weaknesses that apply to you.

TYPICAL STRENGTHS

✔ Bold
✔ Direct
___ Confident
___ Competitive
✔ Pioneering
✔ Assertive
___ Frank
___ Independent
___ Like Challenges
✔ Visionary

TYPICAL WEAKNESSES

✔ Impatient
✔ Insensitive
✔ Dislike Details
✔ Poor Listener
✔ Dictatorial
___ Impulsive
___ Too Blunt
✔ Hate Routines
___ Self-Centered
✔ Overbearing

H W
✔

BALANCED D

NOTE: If your D is in the balanced range, look at **both** the High D and Low D boxes and **husbands check, wives circle** those strengths and weaknesses that apply to you.

H W
✔

LOW D CHARACTERISTICS

OVERVIEW: Low D personalities are motivated to accept the environment rather than control it.

Husbands check, wives circle all the strengths and weaknesses that apply to you.

TYPICAL STRENGTHS

✔ Gentle
___ Tactful
___ Submissive
___ Easygoing
✔ Supportive
___ Sensitive
✔ Harmonious
___ Lenient
___ Mild
___ Cooperative

TYPICAL WEAKNESSES

___ Unassertive
___ Too Sensitive
✔ Underestimate Self
___ Don't Take a Stand
___ Shy
___ Timid
✔ Become Resentful
✔ Lack Confidence
___ Slow to Confront
___ Dependent

INSTRUCTIONS: Mark the boxes in the left hand margin. **Step #1.** Husbands will check the appropriate box in the "H" column, and wives will use the "W" column. **Step #2.** Now mark the strengths and weaknesses in the appropriate box that describes you.

DOMINANT

H   W

HIGH D CHARACTERISTICS

OVERVIEW: High D personalities are naturally motivated to be in control of their environment.

Husbands check, wives circle all the strengths and weaknesses that apply to you.

TYPICAL STRENGTHS   TYPICAL WEAKNESSES

Bold	Assertive	Impatient	Impulsive
Direct	Frank	Insensitive	Too Blunt
Confident	Independent	Dislike Details	Hate Routines
Competitive	Like Challenges	Poor Listener	Self-Centered
Pioneering	Visionary	Dictatorial	Overbearing

H   W

BALANCED D

NOTE: If your D is in the balanced range, look at **both** the High D and Low D boxes and **husbands check, wives circle** those strengths and weaknesses that apply to you.

H   W

LOW D CHARACTERISTICS

OVERVIEW: Low D personalities are motivated to accept the environment rather than control it.

Husbands check, wives circle all the strengths and weaknesses that apply to you.

TYPICAL STRENGTHS   TYPICAL WEAKNESSES

Gentle	Sensitive	Unassertive	Timid
Tactful	Harmonious	Too Sensitive	Become Resentful
Submissive	Lenient	Underestimate Self	Lack Confidence
Easygoing	Mild	Don't Take a Stand	Slow to Confront
Supportive	Cooperative	Shy	Dependent

INSTRUCTIONS: Mark the boxes in the left hand margin. **Step #1.** Husbands will check the appropriate box in the "H" column, and wives will use the "W" column. **Step #2.** Now mark the strengths and weaknesses in the appropriate box that describes you.

INFLUENCING

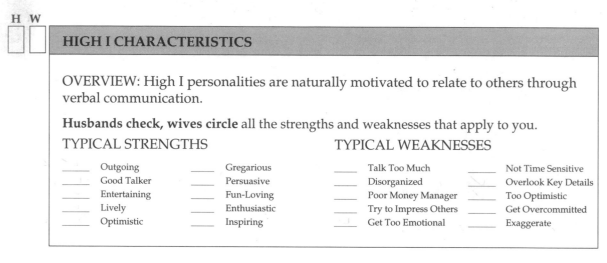

H W

HIGH I CHARACTERISTICS

OVERVIEW: High I personalities are naturally motivated to relate to others through verbal communication.

Husbands check, wives circle all the strengths and weaknesses that apply to you.

TYPICAL STRENGTHS

_____ Outgoing   _____ Gregarious
_____ Good Talker   _____ Persuasive
_____ Entertaining   _____ Fun-Loving
_____ Lively   _____ Enthusiastic
_____ Optimistic   _____ Inspiring

TYPICAL WEAKNESSES

_____ Talk Too Much   _____ Not Time Sensitive
_____ Disorganized   _____ Overlook Key Details
_____ Poor Money Manager   _____ Too Optimistic
_____ Try to Impress Others _____ Get Overcommitted
_____ Get Too Emotional   _____ Exaggerate

H W

BALANCED I

NOTE: If your I is in the balanced range, look at **both** the High I and Low I boxes and **husbands check, wives circle** those strengths and weaknesses that apply to you.

H W

LOW I CHARACTERISTICS

OVERVIEW: Low I personalities are de-energized by a high level of socialization, especially with strangers; consequently, they are motivated to be reserved.

Husbands check, wives circle all the strengths and weaknesses that apply to you.

TYPICAL STRENGTHS

_____ Work Well Alone   _____ Reserved
_____ Focused   _____ Efficient
_____ Realistic   _____ Frugal
_____ Earnest   _____ Reliable
_____ Factual   _____ Don't Exaggerate

TYPICAL WEAKNESSES

_____ Appear Unfriendly   _____ Can Be Harsh
_____ Secretive   _____ Not Transparent
_____ Shy in Public   _____ Tire from Socializing
_____ Pessimistic   _____ Lack Enthusiasm
_____ Don't Share Ideas _____ Not a Team Player

16

INSTRUCTIONS: Mark the boxes in the left hand margin. **Step #1.** Husbands will check the appropriate box in the "H" column, and wives will use the "W" column. **Step #2.** Now mark the strengths and weaknesses in the appropriate box that describes you.

STEADY

H W

HIGH S CHARACTERISTICS

OVERVIEW: High S personalities are naturally motivated to maintain stability and harmony in the environment by cooperating with others.

Husbands check, wives circle all the strengths and weaknesses that apply to you.

TYPICAL STRENGTHS

_____ Harmonious	_____ Peaceful
_____ Good Listener	_____ Considerate
_____ Cooperative	_____ Understanding
_____ Patient	_____ Steady
_____ Supportive	_____ Loyal

TYPICAL WEAKNESSES

_____ Compromise Too Much	_____ Vacillate
_____ Don't Like Change	_____ Get in a Rut
_____ Too Trusting	_____ Naive
_____ Afraid to Confront	_____ Noncommittal
_____ Complacent	_____ Passive

H W

BALANCED S

NOTE: If your S is in the balanced range, look at **both** the High S and Low S boxes and **husbands check, wives circle** those strengths and weaknesses that apply to you.

H W

LOW S CHARACTERISTICS

OVERVIEW: Low S personalities are motivated to change the environment through action or words.

Husbands check, wives circle all the strengths and weaknesses that apply to you.

TYPICAL STRENGTHS

_____ Action-Oriented	_____ Initiating
_____ Energetic	_____ Dynamic
_____ Spontaneous	_____ Flexible
_____ Change-Oriented	_____ Want Variety
_____ Alert	_____ Quick to React

TYPICAL WEAKNESSES

_____ Too Impatient	_____ Not Content
_____ Neglect Commitments	_____ Abrupt
_____ Can't Be Still	_____ Hyperactive
_____ Easily Distracted	_____ Don't Finish Projects
_____ Insensitive	_____ Too Critical

INSTRUCTIONS: Mark the boxes in the left hand margin. **Step #1.** Husbands will check the appropriate box in the "H" column, and wives will use the "W" column. **Step #2.** Now mark the strengths and weaknesses in the appropriate box that describes you.

CONSCIENTIOUS

H W

HIGH C CHARACTERISTICS

OVERVIEW: High C personalities are naturally motivated to be accurate and achieve a high standard of quality in everything undertaken.

Husbands check, wives circle all the strengths and weaknesses that apply to you.

TYPICAL STRENGTHS

Accurate	Thorough
Organized	Analytical
Cautious	Like to Be Prepared
Conscientious	High Standards
Detailed	Focused

TYPICAL WEAKNESSES

Too Picky	Unrealistic Standards
Too Sensitive	Internalize Emotions
Too Cautious	Perfectionist
Cold	Overly Analytical
Rigid	Too Inflexible

H W

BALANCED C

NOTE: If your C is in the balanced range, look at **both** the High C and Low C boxes and **husbands check, wives circle** those strengths and weaknesses that apply to you.

H W

LOW C CHARACTERISTICS

OVERVIEW: Low C personalities are motivated by the opportunity to respond on the spot without extensive preparation.

Husbands check, wives circle all the strengths and weaknesses that apply to you.

TYPICAL STRENGTHS

Independent	Confident
Unconventional	Free-Spirited
Versatile	Generalist
Pragmatic	Good Estimator
Respond Quickly	Good at Impromptu

TYPICAL WEAKNESSES

Disorganized	Unprepared
Unfocused	Overlook Details
Opinionated	Rebellious
Undisciplined	Ignore Rules
Careless	Messy

Continue with 6 . ➡

→ **6** **List Your Key Strengths**

Look back at the strengths you marked on the previous four pages and identify the seven behaviors that represent your strongest personality characteristics. After you have listed the strengths, have your spouse reflect on how each strength will be an asset for your family life.

Husband's Strengths   Wife's Comments

1. _____   _____
2. _____   _____
3. _____   _____
4. _____   _____
5. _____   _____
6. _____   _____
7. _____   _____

In the space below, wives should list any other strengths not mentioned above, again commenting on how each will be an asset to the family.

1. _____   _____
2. _____   _____
3. _____   _____

Wife's Strengths   Husband's Comments

1. _____   _____
2. _____   _____
3. _____   _____
4. _____   _____
5. _____   _____
6. _____   _____
7. _____   _____

In the space below, husbands should list any other strengths not mentioned above, again commenting on how each will be an asset to the family.

1. _____   _____
2. _____   _____
3. _____   _____

→

→ **7** **List Your Key Weaknesses**

Review the weaknesses you marked on the previous pages. In the space below, list the seven most problem areas in your personality profile. After you have listed the weaknesses, have your spouse reflect on how each weakness can be a source of irritation. Prayerfully and humbly approach this step.

Husband's Weaknesses   Wife's Comments

1. _____   _____
2. _____   _____
3. _____   _____
4. _____   _____
5. _____   _____
6. _____   _____
7. _____   _____

In the space below, wives should list any other weaknesses not mentioned above, again commenting on how each can be a source of irritation to the family.

1. _____   _____
2. _____   _____
3. _____   _____

Wife's Weaknesses   Husband's Comments

1. _____   _____
2. _____   _____
3. _____   _____
4. _____   _____
5. _____   _____
6. _____   _____
7. _____   _____

In the space below, husbands should list any other weaknesses not mentioned above, again commenting on how each can be a source of irritation to the family.

1. _____   _____
2. _____   _____
3. _____   _____

→

8 BUILDING TEAMWORK IN YOUR MARRIAGE

One of the exciting steps of building teamwork in your marriage is discovering how you and your spouse can complement each other's weaknesses. Everyone has strengths and weaknesses. Complete the exercises below to build teamwork in your marriage.

FOR THE HUSBAND:

Q: What strengths do you have that can compensate for your spouse's weaknesses?

_____

_____

Q: What weaknesses do you have that make your spouse's strengths helpful?

_____

_____

Q: What combined strengths do you both have?

_____

_____

Q: According to Ephesians 5:25 what did Jesus do for the church in spite of all our weaknesses and failures? What example does this set for husbands?

_____

_____

_____

List below your wife's strengths that will enrich your marriage and for which you are thankful before God.

_____

_____

_____

_____

List the weaknesses in her personality and temperament that irritate you the most.

_____

_____

_____

_____

Will you commit to not nagging or criticizing your wife in these areas but, instead, pray for patience and understanding and for her victory?

_____

Turn the page and continue. ➡️

FOR THE WIFE:

Q: What strengths do you have that can compensate for your spouse's weaknesses?

_____

_____

Q: What weaknesses do you have that make your spouse's strengths helpful?

_____

_____

Q: What combined strengths do you both have?

_____

_____

Q: According to Ephesians 5:33, what attitude should a wife have toward her husband?

_____

_____

Q: How can a wife respect her husband in spite of his weaknesses?

_____

_____

List below your husband's strengths that will enrich your marriage and for which you are thankful before God.

_____

_____

_____

_____

List the weaknesses in his personality and temperament which irritate you the most.

_____

_____

_____

_____

Will you commit to not nagging or criticizing your husband in these areas but, instead, pray for patience and understanding and for his victory?

_____

MARRIAGE DYNAMICS AND "DISC" TENDENCIES

HIGH "D"

Because they are take-charge people, High D personalities tend to exert control over the family life. They are good problem-solvers, independent, respond to new challenges, and create pressure to get results. Watch out—they can be overbearing! If you are a "High D," discuss how you can contribute to your marriage with these elements.

- ** Build
- ** Develop
- ** Create
- ** Decide
- ** Be in control

- ** Direct
- ** Supervise
- ** Lead
- ** Manage
- ** Solve problems

HIGH "I"

Because of their influential nature, High I personalities are very people-oriented. They enjoy entertaining neighbors and guests in the home, variety and spontaneity, and being fun and light-hearted. Watch out—they can be forgetful! If you are a "High I," discuss how you can contribute to your marriage with these elements.

- ** Talk
- ** Influence
- ** Socialize
- ** Initiate new ideas
- ** Be humorous

- ** Entertain
- ** Gain recognition
- ** Relate
- ** Perform
- ** Be active

HIGH "S"

Because they are steady, loyal people, High S personalities bring a calming influence to the home. They excel at cooperating with others, providing security and harmony, and lending a helping hand. Watch out—they may be habitually late! If you are a "High S," discuss how you can contribute to your marriage with these elements.

- ** Create routines
- ** Focus (one task at a time)
- ** Set an example quietly
- ** Be loyal
- ** Follow

- ** Be free from conflict
- ** Support others
- ** Listen and express compassion
- ** Be consistent
- ** Be still

HIGH "C"

Because of their desire to be logical and organized, High C personalities are motivated to be accurate, practical, and thorough. They maintain high expectations, provide structure, and strive for efficiency around the house. Watch out—even though they are frequently right, they may come across as critical or judgmental. If you are a "High C," discuss how you can contribute to your marriage with these elements.

- ** Analyze
- ** Organize
- ** Be thorough
- ** Think and process
- ** Work with things, data

- ** Research facts
- ** Critique and improve
- ** Be accurate
- ** Follow procedures
- ** Plan

The graph you developed on page 11 describes the natural behavior of both the husband and wife. Study the graph carefully and make note of any DISC dimensions that are plotted two or more blocks apart from one another. This dynamic reveals areas in which you and your spouse are most prone to misunderstand one another, due to natural temperament. The greater the divergence, the easier it will be to misunderstand one another.

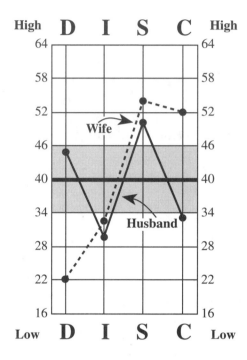

For instance, in the example at left, the wife's graph shows the "D" dimension at 22 (low), but the husband's graph shows the "D" dimension at 45 (balanced). In this example, the husband is more direct, decisive, and bold than his wife's natural behavior. These two will need to clearly discuss areas related to honoring feelings and completing family projects efficiently.

Also, note that the husband's and wife's C points are separated by three blocks, indicating the wife is more detail-oriented, analytical, and eager to establish routines in daily life than her husband. He may feel pressure from his wife because he is not as organized as she naturally is.

Notice also that this couple has very similar scores in the High I and High S dimensions. This suggests that both are steady and reliable in their daily habits, and they put a high priority on maintaining harmony in their relationship.

Couples can discover a new dimension in their Christian service by identifying areas of mutual strength that can be utilized by the Lord. If He has blessed you both with a common strength, has He specially gifted you for a reason ? Do you know what that reason is?

Further, a new dimension of marital growth can result from learning to work as a team by complementing, not criticizing, one another's weaknesses.

INSTRUCTIONS: Return to page 11 and compare your husband and wife graphs. If the DISC points are relatively close, your natural behaviors are typically compatible.

If your husband and wife DISC points are significantly separated (two or more blocks) on the graph, the potential for naturally misunderstanding one another rises. Mark the appropriate boxes on the next page and discuss how you each can modify your behavior to become more sensitive.

→

11 Celebrating Your Temperament Differences

If there is a significant difference in your graph points on page 11 (two or more blocks), check the applicable dimensions below and use them to help you analyze potential stress areas.

D Dimension

If your D points are separated by two or more blocks, the High D may be frustrated by the Low D's slowness and lack of directness. The Low D may perceive the High D as pushy, insensitive, or domineering.

To celebrate your differences, the High D should honor the relational element the Low D brings to the marriage, along with his or her sensitivity to feelings. The Low D, in turn, should honor the High D for force of character, commitment to defining and reaching family goals, and for decisiveness.

I Dimension

If your High I points are separated by two or more blocks, the High I may be frustrated by the Low I's lack of interest in social events, unwillingness to talk, or critical or pessimistic attitude. The Low I, in turn, may be frustrated by the High I's disorganization, lack of attention to detail, emotional outbursts, and constant stream of new ideas.

To celebrate your differences, the High I should honor the stability the Low I brings to the marriage and the need to be alone at times. In turn, the Low I should honor the High I for the contribution to the marriage of creativity, enthusiasm, and a positive outlook.

S Dimension

If your High S points are separated by two or more blocks, the High S may be frustrated by the Low S's impatience, bluntness, insensitivity to people, or lack of follow-through. In turn, the Low S may be frustrated by the High S's sentimentality, naivete, lack of direction, and priority for pleasing others.

To celebrate the differences, the High S should honor the Low S for taking the initiative to make needed changes, a high energy level, and the ability to complete a task. In turn, the Low S should honor the High S for the steady, calming, and caring influence he or she offers that makes a house a home.

C Dimension

If your High C points are separated by two or more blocks, the High C may be frustrated by the Low C's lack of concern for details, lack of discipline, untidy habits, and general disorganization. In turn, the Low C may be frustrated by the High C's cautiousness, unwillingness to take risks, insistence on being right, and sticking to the rules.

To celebrate the differences, the High C should honor the Low C for being able to see the "big picture," decisiveness, and the ability to bring spontaneity to the marriage. In turn, the Low C should honor the High C for the contributions to the marriage of organization, accuracy, and standards.

➡️ HOW TO COMMUNICATE WITH "DISC" PERSONALITIES

One of the most difficult challenges in any family is to have effective communications. By recognizing that each DISC profile is operating from a different perspective, you can tailor your communications accordingly. The following tips will help you to improve your communication with others and help you to understand yourself better.

WHEN COMMUNICATING WITH A

HIGH "D," answer the WHAT question.

When talking with <u>High D personalities,</u> discuss the bottom line first. Don't begin by elaborating on all the details or you will lose their attention. Summarize first, and THEN provide explanations, details, and concerns if they request them. Since they naturally are not good listeners, it often is helpful to put your thoughts on paper, giving the problems, options, and actions recommended.

HIGH "I," answer the WHO question.

Personal testimonies and endorsements usually are effective because <u>High I personalities</u> are motivated to relate to others, especially to those who are recognized and prestigious. Persuade them by relating "who" is involved and "who" thinks it's a good idea. Also show them how the project will be fun and exciting. Give them the big picture, but remind them often of the details, or they will forget.

HIGH "S," answer the HOW question.

<u>High S personalities</u> naturally think of the practical details of any project and want to know the specifics of how things will be done and how it will affect them. Prepare them in advance for changes. Use voice tones and body language that communicate a gentle and non-controversial approach.

HIGH "C," answer the WHY question.

Since they are naturally logical, organized, and accurate, <u>High C personalities</u> tend to resist changes unless they understand the reasons why. Provide the rationale for changes, decisions, or actions through well-researched details, facts, and data. They are motivated by logic, not by feelings and emotions.

ASSIGNMENT: Give a specific example of how these tips can enrich your ability to communicate with each other.

➡️

HOW TO DISAGREE WITH DIFFERENT "DISC" PERSONALITIES

Frequently, good communications are enhanced by our ability to interact with people who see situations differently from the way we do. Comprehending God-given differences in temperaments is an important first step toward conflict resolution at home.

HIGH "D"

FIND THE LARGER GOAL you can agree on first; then propose a plan that will expedite reaching the goal. High D personalities are highly committed to reaching their goals, but the particular methodology is secondary. **EXAMPLE:** "I agree that we need to get out of debt. Look at these adjustments to our monthly budget that will result in being debt-free!"

HIGH "I"

POSTPONE AN IMMEDIATE DECISION if possible. High I personalities are highly committed to their ideas but, with the passing of time, frequently lose their emotional attachment. Delaying the decision for a day or two may open the door for them to accept other new ideas. **EXAMPLE:** "That IS a great idea. I never would have thought of that. Let me think and pray about it for a day or two. Okay?"

HIGH "S"

PROVIDE A SPECIFIC EXAMPLE of how your plan has worked in other settings. Take a team approach and offer reassurance of your relationship. Disagreement with High S personalities likely may be interpreted as a personal rejection. Assurances of being "in this together" enable them to relax and accommodate something new and different. **EXAMPLE:** "Remember the last time you changed jobs? It was scarey at first, but soon you discovered a whole group of new friends. And you can always count on me."

HIGH "C"

Carefully DOCUMENT YOUR POSITION with facts and data that have been well researched, and offer proof. Then ask them to consider the case. Try not to back High C personalities into a corner but, instead, give them time to think about the evidence and appeal to their logic. Avoid public embarrassments and corrections with these individuals who already are striving for exceptional quality and precision. **EXAMPLE:** "These are our fast food receipts for the last four months. Add them up, and see if you don't think we're eating out too much."

ASSIGNMENT: Analyze a recent disagreement between the two of you. Discuss how these tips could have eased the tension.

The following page provides more specific helps on how to resolve conflict with people of differing temperaments.

RESOLVING CONFLICT AMONG "DISC" PERSONALITIES

Many times our conflicts with others are a direct result of differences in our motivated behaviors. Shown below are some typical areas where conflicts occur between various personalities. Review the combinations below and then analyze your inclination to misunderstand those who are different from you. Give special attention to the matchup between you and your spouse.

High D personality conflicts with:

High D. Conflict occurs over control. Turf wars can result unless there are clearly defined territorial lines of authority and respect for one another.

High I. The High D personality is turned off by too much talk and not enough results.

High S. The High D doesn't understand why the High S personality isn't more aggressive.

High C. The High D conflicts with people who try to slow him or her down with technicalities or excessive caution.

Based on what you know about *Dominant* profiles and your own nature, give specific examples of how you are most likely to conflict with High D personalities.

(Husband) _____

_____

(Wife) _____

_____

High I personality conflicts with:

High D. The High I can get offended when the High D doesn't ask for an opinion on important decisions.

High I. The High I can be jealous of someone else having the center of attention (another High I).

High S. The High I gets along pretty well but does see the High S as being too sensitive and slow.

High C. Since the High I is naturally optimistic, there is a high potential for conflict with the more practical but sometimes pessimistic attitude of the High C.

Based on what you know about *Influencing* profiles and your own nature, give specific examples of how you are most likely to conflict with High I personalities.

(Husband) _____

_____

(Wife) _____

_____

High S personality conflicts with:

High D. The High S often doesn't say anything but builds up resentment toward "steamroller" High D personalities, who are viewed as being self-centered and insensitive.

High I. The High S eventually becomes impatient and worn out with the High I who overextends with too much talking and verbal aggression.

High S. The High S usually enjoys being together with other S personalities because they are not a threat; however, they do have difficulty making joint decisions (neither wants to impose on the other).

High C. Generally not a bad match, but the High S personality can sometimes feel judged by the High C.

Based on what you know about *Steady* profiles and your own nature, give specific examples of how you are most likely to conflict with High S personalities.

(Husband) _____

_____

(Wife) _____

High C personality conflicts with:

High D. The High C sometimes sees the D as having a know-it-all attitude. Also, the High C is concerned when he or she sees a D initiating plans without considering the necessary details or following established procedures.

High I. Because they are nearly opposites, the High C notices and is easily turned off to many High I tendencies, including disorganization, inaccuracies, exaggeration, and a show-off attitude.

High S. The High C often sees himself or herself as more productive and more disciplined than his or her High S counterpart.

High C. Like the D with D, the High C tends to have turf wars over who is in control and who is correct.

Based on what you know about *Conscientious* profiles and your own nature, give specific examples of how you are most likely to conflict with High C personalities.

(Husband) _____

_____

(Wife) _____

The Bible offers the best advice concerning relationships and how we are to react to each other. Ephesians chapter 4 is especially encouraging in this area. The basic concept is to love one another and to put others above ourselves. Normally, this is not a natural behavior, but it is the fruit of a Spirit-controlled personality.

DISC DIMENSIONS AND FINANCES

Each DISC dimension brings particular strengths and weaknesses to the task of money management. These strengths are noted below, followed by a summary of typical pitfalls that occur when differing temperaments marry each other.

THE HIGH D AND PERSONAL FINANCES

High D personalities make thrifty shoppers. They go straight to the store, purchase what they want, and go home—slam, dunk!

Because High D personalities respond to new challenges, big-picture thinking, and setting goals, they are particularly equipped to provide direction to a family's long-term financial planning. They excel at withstanding current sacrifice in order to attain goals at a later time.

Weaknesses include becoming too controlling, using money to wield power, greed, overlooking or minimizing current family needs, and failing to be a "team player" by excluding the perspective of the spouse.

A helpful passage to balance these weaknesses comes from 1 Timothy 6:9-10:*"But those who want to get rich fall into temptation and a snare and many foolish and harmful desires which plunge men into ruin and destruction. For the love of money is a root of all sorts of evil, and some by longing for it have wandered away from the faith, and pierced themselves with many a pang."*

Our Career Pathways research indicates that High D personalities are among the strongest money managers, due to their task-orientation and tough-mindedness.

THE HIGH I AND PERSONAL FINANCES

High I personalities see shopping as a social event. Malls teeming with people tempt the High I to escape problems through shopping.

Because High I personalities optimistically envision the future, they bring creative thinking, initiative, and lofty possibilities into the family's financial picture.

Weaknesses include changing plans mid-stream too much, shrugging off the discipline of a budget, impulsive spending, pride, and using money to acquire prestige, approval, recognition, and social status.

A helpful passage to balance these weaknesses comes from Matthew 16:26: *"For what will a man be profited, if he gains the whole world, and forfeits his soul? Or what will a man give in exchange for his soul?"*

Our Career Pathways research shows that a High I may struggle with financial stability due to the weaknesses listed above. As a result, the High I should balance himself or herself with a High D or High C whenever possible.

THE HIGH S AND PERSONAL FINANCES

Shopping for the High S is generally a chore because he or she often procrastinates as long as possible before going and may experience difficulty in making decisions about major purchases.

High S personalities excel as compassionate individuals and are particularly adept at responding to human needs with financial resources. Their desire to help and to please others, however, may lead to financial struggles and perhaps ongoing debt.

Weaknesses include being slow to adapt to new financial challenges, failing to plan for the long-term future, procrastinating with financial decisions, signing security out of obligation to others, and having difficulty in telling salespeople "No."

A helpful passage for the High S comes from Proverbs 6:1-2,5: *"My son, if you become surety for your neighbor, have given a pledge for a stranger, if you have been snared with the words of your mouth . . . Deliver yourself like a gazelle from the hunter's hand, and like a bird from the hand of the fowler."*

Like the High I, our Career Pathways research indicates that the High S is likely to struggle with financial soundness. He or she is prone to being empathetic, giving, relational, and desirous of enjoying comfort in the present moments.

THE HIGH C AND PERSONAL FINANCES

The High C really shops. With calculator in hand, he or she meticulously compares prices to obtain the best deal and insists on quality. Unlike the High S, the High C has no trouble pointing out an error in the checkout line or returning defective merchandise.

With a temperament that is naturally analytical, organized, and detail-oriented, High C personalities excel at keeping financial records. Balancing the checkbook each month is nearly an exercise in self-entertainment for the High C. Financial planning, analyzing financial instruments, and accounting for every penny come naturally to this personality.

Weaknesses include indecision brought on by a preoccupation with analysis, being too rigid and inflexible, having pride in self-sufficiency, and being legalistically correct to the neglect of unplanned family financial needs.

A helpful passage to balance these weaknesses can be found in 1 Corinthians 10:12: *"Therefore let him who thinks he stands take heed lest he fall."*

Our Career Pathways research suggests that the High C tends to be the most financially sound of all four temperaments, the least impulsive, and the least often in debt.

Additional Personality Resources

All the books in this section use the DISC or an equivalent system to explain personality. All are written from a Christian perspective.

Connections, Using Personality Types to Draw Parents & Kids Closer. Jim Brawner with Duncan Jaenicke. Chicago, IL: Moody Press, 1991.

Kids in Sports, Shaping a Child's Character from the Sidelines. Bill Perkins with Rod Cooper. Sisters, OR: Multnomah Press, 1989.

Personality Plus. Florence Littauer. Tarrytown, NY: Fleming H. Revell, 1983.

Personality Puzzle. Florence Littauer and Morita Littauer. Grand Rapids, MI: Fleming H. Revell (Baker Book House), 1992.

Spirit-Controlled Temperament. Tim LaHaye. Wheaton, IL: Tyndale House, 1966.

The Two Sides of Love. Gary Smalley and John Trent. Colorado Springs, CO: Focus on the Family Publishing, 1990.

Understanding How Others Misunderstand You. Ken Voges and Ron Braund. Chicago: Moody Press, 1991. (The workbook by the same name is excellent and contains two Biblical Discernment Inventories.)

Understanding Jesus, A Personality Profile. Ken Voges and Mike Kempainen. Chicago: Moody Press, 1992.

The Winning Hand—Making the Most of Your Family's Personality Differences. Wayne Rickerson. Colorado Springs, CO: NavPress, 1991.

Different Children Different Needs. Charles F. Boyd with David Beohi. Sisters, OR: Multnomah Press, 1994.

A Comparison of Four Dimension Personality Instruments				
System and Author	**D**	**I**	**S**	**C**
Career Pathways, Ellis:	Dominant	Influencing	Steady	Conscientious
DiSC Personal Profile System™ Inventory (©Carlson Learning Company), Geier:	Dominance	Influencing	Steadiness	Cautiousness
Personal DISCernment™ Inventory (©Team Resources Inc.), Mohler:	Dominance	Influence	Steadiness	Compliance
CARD Personality Style, Rickerson:	Dominant D ←	Relational R ←	Amiable A ←	Conscientious C (CARD)
Personal Styles, Merrill/Reid:	Driver	Expressive	Amiable	Analytical
Greek, Hippocrates, LaHaye/Littauer:	Choleric	Sanguine	Phlegmatic	Melancholy
Animal, Smalley/Trent:	Lion	Otter	Golden Retriever	Beaver

CHAPTER 3

Hoarding or Overspending: Discovering Your Tendencies in Money Management

CHAPTER 3

Hoarding or Overspending: Discovering Your Tendencies in Money Management

Money represents economic power that can be abused in at least two ways: hoarding or overspending. Most people have the tendency to lean in one direction or the other.

Hoarding takes responsible saving to the extreme by accumulating far above and beyond what is required for basic needs. Legitimate family needs may be overlooked or neglected when a person has this tendency. This type of individual sometimes is described as tight, stingy, frugal, cheap, or miserly.

Overspending is the opposite extreme, characterized by people who habitually shuffle more money than they have through their accounts. The inability to say "no" to the latest new electronics gadget, toy, or sale at the mall makes the overspender easy prey in today's world of advertising.

As you might imagine, the marriage of a hoarder to an overspender could set the stage for marital stress. Left unresolved, this stress also could become a wedge used by Satan to divide husband and wife.

The following survey will help you and your spouse to identify your money management tendencies. After you have tabulated your results, review how you each marked the questions. This should help you to understand the underlying values you each bring to money management. As mentioned earlier in the personality section, rarely are two people perfectly matched. By discovering your differences in advance, you can begin to see how God has prepared each of you to make unique contributions to your marriage.

FINANCIAL MANAGEMENT SURVEY
Discover Your Tendencies

Directions: Read the following pairs of statements and mark the **one** that best describes your typical financial habits or general attitude in the area of financial management. When applicable, your response should be based on your actual track record and not on what you wish you had done. If you feel that neither choice fits, you should select the response that most closely matches your basic attitude about that issue.

How to Mark Your Response: Please take the survey one at a time. Men, use "X" to mark your responses, and women use "O" to mark your responses. *(Note: You may find it helpful to use different colored ink pens, or one use a pencil and the other a pen. This will facilitate the step of scoring your survey. And remember, "X" for men, "O" is for women.)*

When finished, both of you should have responded once to each pair of statements. It is possible for both of you to mark the same statement. Study the examples below before proceeding.

Left Column   Right Column

EXAMPLE #1

[X] _____ 1. **I set aside savings from each paycheck.**

    [O] _____ Since it takes all I can make to live on, I do not have any savings.

EXAMPLE #2

    [ ] _____ 2. I usually carry over a balance on my credit cards each month.

[XO] _____ **I don't use a credit card, or if I do, I pay the balance in full each month.**

Explanation: In the first example, the man feels as if the first statement best describes himself, and the woman has indicated that the second statement best describes her.

In the second example, both people have indicated the second statement best describes themselves.

Left Column   Right Column

[ ] _____ 1. **I set aside savings from each paycheck.**

    [ ] _____ Since it takes all I can make to live on, I do not have any savings.

    [ ] _____ 2. I usually carry over a balance on my credit cards each month.

[ ] _____ **I don't use a credit card or, if I do I pay the balance in full each month.**

    [ ] _____ 3. I have a hard time figuring out where all my money goes.

[ ] _____ **I know exactly how my money is spent.**

[ ] _____ 4. **I pay all my bills on time.**

    [ ] _____ I am sometimes late in paying my bills.

    [ ] _____ 5. **When I see something I really want, I usually just charge it to my credit card.**

[ ] _____ **I usually put off buying something in order to think about it for a while.**

Left   Right
Column Column

☐ _____ 6. **I have money set aside for paying taxes, repairing the car, or other needs.**

       ☐ _____ I usually have to charge (borrow) to cover unexpected expenditures and then make payments to pay it off.

       ☐ _____ 7. I sometimes borrow money from friends or relatives to get by.

☐ _____ **I never borrow money except to buy a house or a car.**

☐ _____ 8. **I follow a systematic plan for saving money.**

       ☐ _____ It takes all I make to afford my current standard of living.

       ☐ _____ 9. I have difficulty balancing my checkbook.

☐ _____ **I balance my checkbook with my monthly bank statement without any major problems.**

☐ _____ 10. **I am very careful to control my spending.**

       ☐ _____ If I have money available, I usually have something already selected to spend it on.

☐ _____ 11. **I live on a budget.**

       ☐ _____ I don't make enough money (or I make too much money) to worry about budgeting.

       ☐ _____ 12. I tend to buy things that are on sale, even though I don't really need them.

☐ _____ **I try not to buy unnecessary items if I can help it.**

       ☐ _____ 13. My family and friends would say that I am a spender.

☐ _____ **My family and friends would say that I am a saver.**

Left Column   Right Column

☐ ___ 14 If I just made more money, then I could get by.

☐ _____ **I believe most people could get by if they would learn to live on what they make.**

☐ ___ 15. It makes me feel good to buy something new.

☐ _____ **It makes me feel good to save money.**

☐ _____ 16. **I save before I spend.**

☐ ___ I save what I have left over after I spend.

☐ _____ 17. **I save because money provides security.**

☐ ___ I plan to start a savings program when I get better off financially.

☐ ___ 18. I could care less about having a lot of money.

☐ _____ **It's very important for me to have money.**

☐ _____ 19. **It's more important to save money.**

☐ ___ It's more important for me to live comfortably.

☐ ___ 20. I sometimes pay a charge for overdrawing my checking account.

☐ _____ **I never write checks unless I have sufficient funds in my account.**

☐ ___ 21. Having a new car, a lot of clothes, and a nice house is more important to me.

☐ _____ **Staying out of debt is more important to me.**

☐ ___ 22. It's really more like me to be generous with my money.

☐ _____ **It's really more like me to be stingy with my money.**

Left   Right
Column   Column

☐ ____ 23. I have some debts, but that's normal in today's society.

☐ _____ **I would rather live in a shack and wear used clothes than have debts.**

☐ _____ 24. **I have a strong desire to be wealthy.**

☐ _____ I don't worry about how much money I have.

☐ _____ 25. **I believe people have to accumulate wealth to live successfully.**

☐ _____ I like to have nice things, but I could care less about accumulating money.

☐ ____ 26. Having nice clothes and driving a new car are part of my lifestyle.

☐ _____ **It's more important to save my money than to have nice things.**

☐ _____ 27. **As a young person I had my own saving account and regularly put aside money from my own earnings.**

☐ _____ I usually spent my earnings and was not able to save any.

☐ _____ 28. **When I graduated from high school and started college, I had some of my own money set aside for my education.**

☐ _____ I had no money set aside from my personal earnings when I graduated.

☐ ____ 29. As a young person, I was pretty carefree with my money and never seemed to have enough.

☐ _____ **As a young person, I was generally frugal with my money and usually had some stashed away for things I really needed.**

Left   Right
Column   Column

☐ _____ 30. While growing up, I purchased a lot of things that were fads and later realized I really didn't need them.

☐ _____ **While growing up, I generally avoided the fads and stuck to the basics.**

SCORING YOUR SURVEY

Your answers to the survey are arranged to fall into two columns: Left and Right. Each of you total your responses in each column and record your totals below. Then subtract the total of the Right column from the total in the Left column. (Note: you may end up with a negative number). Then plot your number on the scale below.

	HIS (X)	HERS (O)	EXAMPLE
TOTAL RESPONSES, LEFT COLUMN	_____	_____	10
TOTAL RESPONSES, RIGHT COLUMN	_____	_____	–20
GRAND TOTAL	_____	_____	–10

Now plot your net totals on the scale below.

OVERSPENDER			BALANCED			HOARDER
–25	–15	–5	0	5	15	25

Although people may be relatively balanced in their money management, most have a clear tendency toward either overspending or hoarding. The results from the survey above will provide excellent opportunities for the two of you to discuss your tendencies, as well as how you will begin to function as a financial team after marriage. Review a description of the extremes below and carefully note the characteristics that apply to each of you.

Characteristics of an Overspender

From my experience, overspenders usually don't have well-defined financial goals. As a result, they seldom have a clear plan of action for financial management; instead, they prefer to be more spontaneous or impulsive. As a result, the life of an overspender is often chaotic and is marked by a series of financial emergencies and euphoric, gleeful purchases.

Often overspenders are too optimistic in projecting how far their money will go. They often think in terms of how much the payment for something will be rather than counting the whole cost in light of established financial goals.

There are a number of spiritual issues that can give rise to a lifestyle of overspending. Study the Scripture passages listed below to discover what God's Word says about the spiritual dimensions of overspending.

James 4:1–4 (greed)

_____

_____

Proverbs 25:28 (lack of self-control)

_____

_____

1 Timothy 6:17–19 (pride)

_____

_____

Psalm 37:1–6 (lack of faith)

_____

_____

1 John 2:15–17 (lust)

_____

_____

1 Timothy 6:3–8 (lack of contentment)

_____

_____

Characteristics of a Hoarder

Hoarders are just as compulsive about saving as spenders are about spending. You can see how being married to someone of the opposite extreme is a prescription for ongoing marital conflict. Because hoarders often are driven by a fear of not having enough money, they try to hang on to every penny. Frequently they have an unrealistic financial plan of setting aside as much money as possible, which may result in the neglect of daily needs. Finding the absolute best bargain on an item before purchasing it may become an obsession.

Like the overspender, a number of spiritual issues can feed a lifestyle of hoarding. Study the Scripture passages below to discover what God's Word says about the spiritual dimensions of hoarding.

Matthew 6:25–34 (fear)

_____

_____

Luke 12:15–21 (pride)

_____

_____

Philippians 4:11–13 (lack of faith)

_____

_____

Ephesians 5:3 (greed)

_____

_____

1 Timothy 6:9–10 (love of money)

_____

_____

Learning to Work as a Team

You and your spouse probably will bring may differences to your marriage. The Couples Communication Survey helped you to identify your personality differences, and the Financial Management Survey above has helped you to see your differences in money management tendencies. You also have other differences: the roles for a husband and wife you learned in your own family, the natural gender differences between a male and female, the different socioeconomic backgrounds, and the different educational experiences. In fact, you may have become alarmed about how different the two of you really are.

Not to worry. One of the mysteries of marriage is how beautifully God can weave two different lives into one pattern of unity that reflects His glory. There are two critical dimensions to achieving this unity: a spiritual dimension and a practical "what to do after we've prayed together" dimension.

The first step toward building teamwork and unity in your marriage is to honor a clear commitment to the Lord Jesus Christ. Only He can free you from bondage to your selfish desires and wants. And frankly, many marriages fail these days due to pure selfishness. If you're approaching marriage by only considering what the other person will do for you, you're headed for trouble. John 3:16 reminds us that the heart of loving is giving. If you're not willing to give freely to your future mate, perhaps you should reconsider getting married.

Only Jesus can enable you to fully love one another and to cherish each other in marriage. And even though you cannot make another person love you, you can live your life under the Lordship of Jesus Christ. Just like the diagram below portrays, as each of you grows personally in Christ, you also will find yourselves growing closer in intimacy.

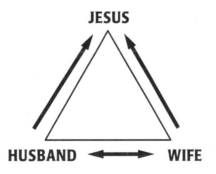

The second step in learning to work as a team is to commit to live by a budget. A planned approach to govern your future spending can bring balance and compromise to your money management. Of course, in the midst of all your wedding preparations, it's hard to sit down and consider all the details surrounding a budget. In fact, the very word *budget* may be unpleasant to your ears.

However, I can promise you this without exception: If you do not live on a budget, you are not handling your finances properly. And if you choose not to live on a budget, I promise you that one of you will be hurt emotionally later in your life. Don't minimize the importance of getting your financial act together through the use of a budget. In my years of counseling, I have found that the stress caused by differences in money management is one of the common reasons couples argue, sometimes driving them to the brink of divorce.

If you plan to marry an overspender, a budget can help restrain that spending impulse and save you from the miseries of debt. On the other hand, if you plan to marry someone who resembles a hoarder, a budget can breathe more flexibility into your family's spending, thus defusing potential arguments and power struggles over money.

Everyone has a plan for spending money. Not having an organized plan is still a plan. In other words, you may choose to be chaotic, disorganized, and painfully ridden by debt, but that is still a plan. A budget is simply an *organized plan* that outlines how you intend to manage your annual income, divided into twelve manageable portions (one for each month).

The next sections of this workbook will help you to draft your budget prior to your marriage. For specific training helps in how to keep your checkbook and an actual system for maintaining your budget and financial records, let me encourage you to obtain a copy of *The Financial Planning Organizer* (Moody Press). It offers specific worksheets that will train you to organize your finances, balance your checkbook, and keep track of your savings.

CHAPTER 4

Creating Your First Budget

CHAPTER 4

Creating Your First Budget

Section One

THE GOAL: LIVING WITHIN YOUR MEANS

L iving *within* your means translates to spending no more than you make on a monthly basis. Ideally, that means living on a cash basis and not using credit or borrowed money to provide normal living expenses. It also means having the self-discipline to control spending and to keep needs, wants, and desires in their proper relationship.

There are two other alternatives. Some people choose to live *above* their means. This involves consistently spending more than they earn—a lifestyle financed by habitual borrowing. Ultimately what is borrowed must be repaid, and unfortunately this often leads to marital stress and even divorce.

Others choose to live *at* their level of means, which basically involves spending everything they earn. The flaw of this lifestyle is that no provision is made for emergencies. Cars break down, unplanned pregnancies occur, and unexpected medical bills are some of the more common problems that can "torpedo" a couple's finances.

The real issue is not how others live, but how you plan to live after you're married. Discuss the kind of lifestyle you plan, and check the appropriate statement below that you are willing to commit to.

_____ We plan to live within our means.   Date _____

_____ We plan to live at our means.   Date _____

_____ We plan to live above our means.   Date _____

To help you manage your spending, rather than vice versa, you will need to wisely categorize your spending in one of three areas:

NEEDS	WANTS	DESIRES
These are the purchases necessary to provide your basic requirements, such as food, clothing, home, medical coverage, and others.	Wants involve choices about the quality of goods to be used. Dress clothes vs. work clothes, steak vs. hamburger, a new car vs. a used car.	These are choices that can be made only out of surplus funds after all other obligations have been met.

Obstacles to Good Money Management

- Yielding to social pressure to own more "things" soon after marriage.
- Having the attitude that "more is better," regardless of the cost.
- Using credit cards to purchase what you cannot pay for.
- Having no savings available to cope with rising prices and unexpected expenses.
- Abandoning initial budgeting plans because of discouragement
- Allowing legalism to make the budget a family weapon instead of a family tool.

The Quick-Fix Answer

You're in danger when income barely equals outgo. Most people try to quick-fix the problem by taking a second or third job, often at the expense of family time. The wiser solution is to regain control by reducing expenditures below your income.

Parts of a Plan to Manage Your Money

In order to consistently live within your means, you need a systematic plan for managing your money called a **budget**. The Bible has key insights for you to follow when you plan your budget.

- The first part belongs to God. It is returned to Him as a tithe in recognition that He owns all we have. We are merely stewards.

"Will a man rob God? Yet you are robbing me! But you say, 'How have we robbed Thee?' In tithes and offerings" (Malachi 3:8).

- The government will take its share.

"Then He said to them, 'Then render to Caesar the things that are Caesar's; and to God the things that are God's'" (Matthew 22:21).

The portion of money available after tithe and taxes is termed *Net Spendable Income (NSI)*.

- Family needs come next.

"But if anyone does not provide for his own, and especially for those of his household, he has denied the faith, and is worse than an unbeliever" (1 Timothy 5:8).

- God says to pay your debts.

"The wicked borrows and does not pay back, but the righteous is gracious and gives" (Psalm 37:21).

- Faithful management yields a fifth portion called the surplus. The creation of surplus should be a major goal for the Christian because it allows us to respond to the needs of others.

"At this present time your abundance being a supply for their want, that their abundance also may become a supply for your want, that there may be equality" (2 Corinthians 8:14).

Even if you are not in debt, in order to maximize the surplus you should manage your finances with a budget.

Figure 4.0

Section Two

WHERE ARE WE?
A FINANCIAL QUESTIONNAIRE

Use the form below to accurately identify all your existing debts. Not only will this information be necessary to the creation of your first budget, it also will ensure that there are no surprises (save those for birthdays and Christmas!).

List all debts and obligations to the nearest whole dollar amount and the associated monthly payment. If the payment is past due, make a note of it. Be sure to list personal or family loans.

HIS			HERS	
Amount owed	Payment		Amount owed	Payment
_____	_____	**Car**	_____	_____
_____	_____	**Clothes**	_____	_____
_____	_____	**Credit Cards**	_____	_____
_____	_____	**School loans**	_____	_____
_____	_____	**Medical**	_____	_____
_____	_____	**Insurance**	_____	_____
_____	_____	**Taxes**	_____	_____
_____	_____	**Loans**	_____	_____
_____	_____	**Child Support**	_____	_____
_____	_____	**Other**	_____	_____

Total Debt	Total Monthly Debt Payments		Total Debt	Total Monthly Debt Payments
_____	_____		_____	_____

Section Three

CATEGORIES FOR YOUR NEW BUDGET

To help you create your first budget together, I have organized a typical family's expenditures into 15 categories. A 16th category has been added to track unallocated surplus income. Take the next few minutes to become acquainted with the various budget categories. An example is provided at the end of this section to illustrate how one family organized their budget.

Determining Income Per Month

List all gross income (income before deductions) in the "Gross Income Per Month" section on the Monthly Income and Expenses Sheet (yours is labeled Form 2 on page 99). Don't forget to include commissions, bonuses, tips, and interest earned that will be received over the next 12 months.

Budgeting on a Variable Income

One of the most difficult problems in budgeting is how to allocate monthly spending when your income fluctuates, as it often does on commission sales. The normal tendency is to spend the money as it comes in. This works great during the high income months but usually causes havoc during the lower income months.

Two suggestions will help anyone living on a fluctuating income: First, always separate any business-related expenses, such as car maintenance, meals, or living accommodations from your normal household expenses. I recommend a separate checking account and separate credit cards for business expenses.

Second, you need to estimate what your (low) average income for one year will be, and generate your monthly budget based on the average income per month. As the funds come in, deposit them in a special savings account and draw a salary from the account. The effect is to ration the income over the year in relatively equal amounts that can be budgeted.

Remember that if you are self-employed you will need to budget for payroll taxes on a quarterly basis. Failure to do this will result in a rather unpleasant visit with representatives of the Internal Revenue Service.

If you are beginning your budget during one of the lower income months, you may have to delay funding of some of the variable expenses like clothing, vacations, or dental bills. These can be funded later, following your honeymoon and when income allows.

Business expense reimbursements should not be considered family income. Avoid the trap of using expense money to buffer family spending, or the result will be an indebtedness that cannot be paid.

What Is Net Spendable Income?

Net Spendable Income is the portion available for family spending. Some of your income doesn't belong to the family and therefore cannot be spent. Note the following.

CATEGORY 1—THE TITHE: Since the term tithe means "a tenth," I will assume that you give 10 percent of your total income to God. For a detailed discussion on the tithe, see *Your Finances in Changing Times* (Moody Press), chapter 10, "Sharing—God's Way."

CATEGORY 2—TAXES: Federal withholding, Social Security, and state and local taxes also must be deducted from gross income. Self-employed individuals must not forget to set aside money for quarterly prepayments on taxes. Beware of the tendency to treat unpaid tax money as windfall profit.

OTHER DEDUCTIONS: Payroll deductions for insurance, credit union savings or debt payments, bonds, stock programs, retirement, and union dues can be handled in either of two ways:

1. Treat them as a deduction from gross income the same as the income taxes.
2. Include them in spendable income and deduct them in the proper category. This is preferred because it provides a more accurate picture of where your money is being spent.

EXAMPLE: A deduction is being made for credit union savings. This amount should be considered as a part of income with an expense shown under category 10, Savings, for the same amount. This method makes it easier to see the overall effect the deduction has on the family budget.

Net Spendable Income = GROSS INCOME MINUS TITHE AND MINUS TAXES.

How Will Your Net Spendable Income Be Spent After Marriage?

CATEGORY 3—HOUSING EXPENSES: All monthly expenses necessary to operate the home include taxes, insurance, maintenance, and utilities. The amount used for utility payments should be an average monthly amount (the previous owner or apartment management can estimate this). If you rent, be sure to secure renter's insurance. If you own but cannot establish an accurate maintenance expense, use 5 percent of the monthly mortgage payment.

CATEGORY 4—FOOD EXPENSES: All grocery expenses include paper goods and non-food products normally purchased at grocery stores. In addition to regular shopping trips, include milk, bread, and items purchased. *Do not include* eating out and daily lunches eaten away from home. To establish an accurate record of food expenses, keep a detailed spending record for the first two months after you're married.

CATEGORY 5—AUTOMOBILE EXPENSES: This includes payments, insurance, gas, oil, maintenance, and depreciation. Maintenance/Repair/Replace is actually the money set aside to repair or replace your automobile(s). The minimum amount set aside should be sufficient to keep the car in decent repair and to replace it at least every four to five years. If the replacement funds are not available in your new budget, the minimum should be maintenance costs. Annual or semi-annual auto insurance payments should be set aside on a monthly basis, thereby avoiding the crisis of a neglected expense.

CATEGORY 6—INSURANCE: Include all insurance, such as health, life, and disability, but not associated with the home or auto.

CATEGORY 7—DEBTS: Include all monthly payments required to meet debt obligations. Home mortgage and automobile payments are not included here.

CATEGORY 8—ENTERTAINMENT AND RECREATION: Vacation savings, camping trips, sporting equipment, hobby expenses, and athletic events are included. Don't forget eating out. I suggest you use the *Cash Organizer*, particularly with this category.

CATEGORY 9—CLOTHING: Divide the average annual amount spent on clothes by 12. The minimum amount should be at least $10 per month per family member.

CATEGORY 10—SAVINGS: Every family should allocate something for savings. A savings account can provide funds for emergencies and is a key element in good planning and financial freedom.

CATEGORY 11—MEDICAL EXPENSES: This includes insurance deductibles, doctors' bills, eyeglasses, drugs, or orthodontist visits. Use a yearly average divided by 12 to determine a monthly amount.

CATEGORY 12—MISCELLANEOUS: Include specific expenses that do not seem to fit anywhere else: pocket allowance (coffee money), miscellaneous gifts, Christmas presents, toiletries, haircuts. Miscellaneous spending is usually underestimated. To establish accurate spending habits, you likely will need to monitor this category carefully in the first two months of your marriage. Again, using the *Cash Organizer* will help. Self-discipline is the key to controlling miscellaneous spending.

CATEGORY 13—INVESTMENTS: If you will have surplus income in your first budget, you can use this category to invest for retirement or other long-term goals. As debt-free status is achieved, more money can be diverted to this category.

CATEGORY 14—SCHOOL/CHILD CARE: If you are marrying someone who has children, use this category. Other budget categories must be reduced to provide these funds.

CATEGORY 15—ALIMONY/CHILD SUPPORT: Use this category if you marry someone with these obligations. Other categories will have to be reduced, however, to make these funds available.

CATEGORY 16—UNALLOCATED SURPLUS INCOME: Income from unbudgeted sources (garage sales, bonuses, gifts) can be kept in a checking account and placed in this category. This section can be useful to keep track of surplus income, as well as to keep records for tax purposes.

INCOME VERSUS EXPENSES

STEP ONE: Compile the expenses under each of the major categories (items 3 through 15) and note this as your total expenses. Then in the space provided subtract expenses from your Net Spendable Income.

STEP TWO: *If income is greater than expenses,* you need only to control spending to maximize your surplus. This money can be used to meet the needs of others and/or for increasing your savings.

STEP THREE: *If expenses are greater than income*, study the guideline budget in the next section.

Study the Sample Budget

To help draft your new budget, study how one family accomplished the task (see Figure 4.1, 4.3). The figures are based on an annual gross income of $25,000, amounting to $2,083 per month. Since your annual income likely will not be precisely $25,000, your monthly allotments will differ. Like the example, however, you will organize your expenditures into the same categories.

HOW ONE FAMILY ORGANIZED THEIR MONTHLY INCOME & EXPENSES

GROSS INCOME PER MONTH $2,083

Salary	2,083
Interest	
Dividends	
Other	

LESS:

1. Tithe   208

2. Tax (Est. - Incl. Fed., State, FICA)   406

NET SPENDABLE INCOME   1,469

3. Housing   560

Mortgage (rent)	350
Insurance (renter's)	30
Taxes	
Electricity	60
Gas	40
Water	15
Sanitation	10
Telephone	30
Maintenance	25
Other	

4. Food   177

5. Automobile(s)   221

Payments	100
Gas & Oil	50
Insurance	40
License/Taxes	6
Maint./Repair/Replace	25

6. Insurance   73

Life	14
Medical	59
Other	

7. Debts   73

Credit Card	73
Loans & Notes	
Other or to Savings	

8. Enter. & Recreation   73

Eating Out	30
Activities/Trips	23
Vacation	20
Other	

9. Clothing   73

10. Savings   73

11. Medical Expenses   73

Doctor	30
Dentist	15
Drugs	28
Other	

12. Miscellaneous   73

Toiletry, cosmetics	10
Beauty, barber	15
Laundry, cleaning	15
Allowances, lunches	15
Gifts (incl. Christmas)	18
Cash	
Other	

13. Investments   0

14. School/Child Care [1]   0

Tuition	
Materials	
Transportation	
Day Care	

15. Alimony/child support [1]   0

TOTAL EXPENSES   1,469

INCOME VS. EXPENSES

Net Spendable Income	1,469
Less Expenses	1,469
	0

16. Unallocated Surplus Income [2]   _____

[1] Categories 14 and 15 should be used if you marry someone who already has children. See Figure 4.2.

[2] This category is used when surplus income is received. This would be kept in the checking account to be used within a few weeks; otherwise, it should be transferred to an allocated category.

Figure 4.1

Section Four

THE GUIDELINE BUDGET

A guideline budget divides family spending into percentages to help determine the *proper balance* in each category of the budget, e.g., Housing, Food, and Automobile. The primary use of the guideline budget is to *indicate problem areas. It is not an absolute.* The percentages shown in Figure 4.2 are based on a family of two with income(s) ranging from $15,000 to $65,000 per year.

About the Guideline Percentages

Newlyweds can range from high school sweethearts, starting with very little financial reserves, to middle-aged adults with substantial reserves. You may need to adjust the percentages in Figure 4.2 to accommodate your specific situation.

For instance, young newlyweds earning $25,000 annually and renting an apartment may not need 38 percent of their income for housing. Instead, they may choose to reduce that percentage and accelerate their savings rate in order to purchase their first home. Middle-aged home owners may want to retain that housing percentage but reduce the amount of entertainment and recreation they enjoy.

Purpose of a Guideline Budget

The percentage guideline is developed to determine a standard against which to compare present spending patterns. It will serve as a basis for determining areas of overspending that are creating the greatest problems. Additionally, it helps to determine where adjustments need to be made. If you are overspending, the percentage guideline can be used as a goal in future budgeting. Although the percentages are guides only and *not* absolute, they do help to establish upper levels of spending.

Let's say a family is spending 40 percent or more of their Net Spendable Income on housing; they will have difficulty balancing their budget. There is little flexibility in most family incomes to absorb excessive spending on housing (or automobiles).

Calculating the Guideline Percentages

Notice that the *Net Spendable Income* (NSI), not the gross income, is used to calculate the ideal spending for each budget category. NSI is determined by subtracting your tithe and taxes from your gross income. If taxes are known, then actual amounts can be used. For example, a married couple with an income of $25,000 per year will pay approximately 19.3 percent of their gross income in taxes (using 1995 tax tables).

In the example shown in Figure 4.3 on page 94, Net Spendable Income is $1,465. Thus for housing, 38 percent of NSI equals $560 per month. Therefore, no more than $560 per month should be spent for housing; this includes payment, taxes, utilities, and upkeep.

Note that in some categories absolutes are impossible because of variables like utilities and taxes. You must adjust percentages within ranges under "Housing," "Food," and "Auto." Those three categories combined cannot exceed 65 percent of your NSI. Example: If 40 percent is used for Housing, the percentage for Food and Auto must be reduced.

Two other categories that defy absolutes are Insurance and Investments, and I will discuss them both in the next section called "Long-Range Planning."

PERCENTAGE GUIDE FOR FAMILY INCOME
(Family of Two)

Gross Income	15,000	25,000	35,000	45,000	55,000	65,000
1. Tithe	10%	10%	10%	10%	10%	10%
2. Taxes [1]	13.4%	19.3%	22%	23%	26%	28.5%
NET SPENDABLE INCOME [2]	11,490	17,675	23,800	30,153	35,200	39,975
3. Housing	38%	38%	34%	30%	27%	26%
4. Food	15%	12%	12%	12%	11%	10%
5. Auto	15%	15%	12%	12%	12%	11%
6. Insurance	5%	5%	5%	5%	5%	5%
7. Debts	5%	5%	5%	5%	5%	5%
8. Ent./Recreation	4%	5%	6%	6%	7%	7%
9. Clothing	4%	5%	5%	5%	6%	6%
10. Savings	5%	5%	5%	5%	5%	5%
11. Medical/Dental	5%	5%	4%	4%	4%	4%
12. Miscellaneous	4%	5%	5%	7%	7%	8%
13. Investments [3]	—	—	7%	9%	11%	13%
14. School/Child Care [4]	—	—	—	—	—	—
15. Alimony/Child Support [4]	—	—	—	—	—	—
16. Unalloc. Surplus Inc. [5]	—	—	—	—	—	—

[1] Guideline percentages for tax category include taxes for Social Security, federal, and a small estimated amount for state, based on 1995 rates. At the $15,000 level of income, the Earned Income Credit drastically reduces the tax burden. However, you must have children to qualify.

[2] Begin figuring 100% from your Net Spendable Income, *not* your Gross Income. Categories 3-13 should total 100% of your Net Spendable Income. On this chart, Larry assumes that couples with incomes below $35,000 probably will not be making investments.

[3] This category is used for long-term investment planning, such as college education or retirement.

[4] This category should be used if you marry someone who already has children. If you have this expense, the percentage shown must be deducted from other budget categories.

[5] This category is used when surplus income is received. This would be kept in the checking account to be used within a few weeks; otherwise, it should be transferred to an allocated category.

Figure 4.2

BUDGET PERCENTAGE GUIDELINES

Salary for guideline = $25,000 /year

Gross Income Per Month $2083

1.	Tithe	(10% of Gross)	(2083)	= $	208
2.	Tax	(19.3% of Gross)	(2083)	= $	406

Net Spendable Income   (1465)

3.	Housing	(38% of Net)	(1465)	= $	560
4.	Food	(12% of Net)	(1465)	= $	177
5.	Auto	(15% of Net)	(1465)	= $	221
6.	Insurance	(5% of Net)	(1465)	= $	73
7.	Debts	(5% of Net)	(1465)	= $	73
8.	Entertain. & Rec.	(5% of Net)	(1465)	= $	73
9.	Clothing	(5% of Net)	(1465)	= $	73
10.	Savings	(5% of Net)	(1465)	= $	73
11.	Medical	(5% of Net)	(1465)	= $	73
12.	Miscellaneous	(5% of Net)	(1465)	= $	73
13.	Investments	(0% of Net)[1]		= $	
14.	School/ Child Care	(8% of Net)[2]		= $	
15.	Alimony/Child Support[2]			= $	

Total   (Cannot exceed Net Spendable Income) $ 1469

16. Unallocated Surplus Income[3]   N/A   = $ _____

[1] Note: considering the given obligations at this income level, there is no surplus for investing long term.

[2] Note: this percentage has *not* been factored into the total percentages shown for net income.

[3] Note: this category is not part of the budget system but can be used to record and show disbursements of unallocated surplus income. This also provides a good record of income for tax purposes.

Figure 4.3

Section Five

LONG-RANGE PLANNING

My advice for newlyweds on the topic of long-range planning can be summed up in one word: *balance*. I typically see two mistakes from young couples in this area. On the one hand, a partner becomes too aggressive and unrealistic when saving toward long-range goals, resulting in family needs being overlooked. Being too stingy with monthly cash flow can create a great deal of marital stress.

On the other hand, I've seen both partners fail to take responsibility for future planning because they are so overwhelmed with debt. And without a specific strategy to retire existing debt, little progress is made, resulting in even more debt.

The key word is balance. While exact circumstances will vary, every couple should record some initial long-range plans for their financial future. These plans should address the following three areas: a strategy for debt retirement; obtaining insurance coverage; and a retirement strategy.

A Strategy for Debt Retirement: Where Should You Start?

The three most common debt traps for newlyweds are school loans, car loans, and outstanding credit card balances. Debt retirement must take priority over insurance and investments for the following reason. What good does it do to contribute money to a retirement plan that earns 8 to 10 percent interest when you are paying 19 to 21 percent interest on your credit card balances?

As a plan of attack, I suggest you organize your debt retirement in the following priority order.

- Start by eliminating the debts that charge you the highest interest rates. These may be credit card balances or consumer loans. Eliminate these accounts first by starting with the least amount first. As each account is paid off, use the payment money to apply to the next least account, and so forth, until all of your highest interest loans are paid back.
- Next, pay off your car loans, followed by any outstanding student loans you have.
- If you're already purchasing a house, make it the final repayment item.

Obtaining Insurance: How Much Is Enough?

Because most newlyweds are operating on limited incomes, I almost always encourage the purchase of "term" insurance. It offers the most coverage for the least amount of dollars.

As a general rule, the amount of coverage to purchase hinges on the amount of income you are seeking to replace in the event your spouse dies. If you do not have children or stepchildren, you should minimally obtain enough life insurance to cover the cost of a funeral in your area of the country. If you are purchasing your home, you might consider also obtaining enough coverage to pay off the mortgage, since life insurance is generally cheaper than mortgage insurance.

The time to reevaluate your coverage is when you begin having children or if your wife chooses to remain at home. A good rule of thumb in those cases is to purchase coverage equal to ten times the amount of your annual income. In the event of your untimely death, the death benefit is usually sufficient to maintain your current income level when it is wisely invested.

The Priority of Retirement

I do not recommend investing for retirement until all of your debts are paid, including your house. As I mentioned before, it does no good to save at the rate of 8 to 10 percent while you're paying interest at a much higher rate.

Generally, couples do not actively begin retirement savings until they are in their early forties or until their debts are all paid. You'll notice from the guideline budgets provided in Figure 4.2, I don't even recommend investments until a family of two reaches the $35,000 annual income level and then only if their debts are paid.

Choosing to defer retirement plans until you are debt-free or until you're in your early forties is a strategy, even though you're not actively saving. *Not* spending money on investments (a retirement plan) releases monthly cash flow to meet more pressing debt-retirement plans.

Getting Started on Your Budget

Having considered the components of a family budget, the next step is to actually draft your first budget. Use the forms provided in the next section (Forms 1, 2, 3) to help you make the calculations.

Section Six

Begin Now

DETERMINE YOUR
BUDGET PERCENTAGE GUIDELINES

Salary for guideline = _____ /year

Gross Income Per Month _____

   1. Tithe   (__ % of Gross) (_____) = $ _____

   2. Tax   (__ % of Gross) (_____) = $ _____

Net Spendable Income   _____

   3. Housing   (__ % of Net)   (_____) = $ _____

   4. Food   (__ % of Net)   (_____) = $ _____

   5. Auto   (__ % of Net)   (_____) = $ _____

   6. Insurance   (__ % of Net)   (_____) = $ _____

   7. Debts   (__ % of Net)   (_____) = $ _____

   8. Entertain.   (__ % of Net)   (_____) = $ _____
       & Rec.

   9. Clothing   (__ % of Net)   (_____) = $ _____

  10. Savings   (__ % of Net)   (_____) = $ _____

  11. Medical   (__ % of Net)   (_____) = $ _____

  12. Miscellaneous (__ % of Net)   (_____) = $ _____

  13. Investments (__ % of Net)   (_____) = $ _____

  14. School/   (__ % of Net)   (_____) = $ _____
       Child Care

  15. Alimony/   (__ % of Net)   (_____) = $ _____
       Child Support

Total (Cannot exceed Net Spendable Income) $ _____

  16. Unallocated Surplus Income   (__N/A__) = $ _____

FORM 1

ORGANIZING YOUR
MONTHLY INCOME & EXPENSES

GROSS INCOME PER MONTH _____

    Salary _____

    Interest _____

    Dividends _____

    Other _____

LESS:

1. **Tithe** _____

2. **Tax** (Est. - Incl. Fed., State, FICA) _____

    NET SPENDABLE INCOME _____

3. **Housing** _____

    Mortgage (rent) _____

    Insurance _____

    Taxes _____

    Electricity _____

    Gas _____

    Water _____

    Sanitation _____

    Telephone _____

    Maintenance _____

    Other _____

4. **Food** _____

5. **Automobile(s)** _____

    Payments _____

    Gas & Oil _____

    *Insurance _____

    *License/Taxes _____

    *Main./Repair/Replace _____

6. **Insurance** _____

    *Life _____

    *Medical _____

    Other _____

7. **Debts** _____

    Credit Card _____

    Loans & Notes _____

    Other _____

8. **Enter. & Recreation** _____

    Eating Out _____

    Activities/Trips _____

    *Vacation _____

    Other _____

*9. **Clothing** _____

10. **Savings** _____

11. **Medical Expenses** _____

    *Doctor _____

    *Dentist _____

    Drugs _____

    Other _____

12. **Miscellaneous** _____

    Toiletry, cosmetics _____

    Beauty, barber _____

    Laundry, cleaning _____

    Allowances, lunches _____

    Subscriptions _____

    Gifts (incl. Christmas) _____

    Cash _____

    Other _____

13. **Investments** _____

14. **School/Child Care** _____

    Tuition _____

    Materials _____

    Transportation _____

    Day Care _____

15. **Alimony/Child Support** _____

TOTAL EXPENSES _____

INCOME VS. EXPENSES

    Net Spendable Income _____

    Less Expenses _____

    _____

16. **Unallocated Surplus Income** [1] _____

[1] This category is used when surplus income is received. This would be kept in the checking account to be used within a few weeks; otherwise, it should be transferred to an allocated category.

* Use the Variable Expense Planning Sheet on the next page to calculate this amount.

FORM 2

VARIABLE EXPENSE PLANNING

Plan for those expenses that are not paid on a regular monthly basis by estimating the yearly cost and determining the monthly amount needed to be set aside for that expense. A helpful formula is to allow the previous year's expense and add 5 percent.

	Estimated Cost		Per Month
1. VACATION	$ _____	÷ 12 =	$ _____
2. DENTIST	$ _____	÷ 12 =	$ _____
3. DOCTOR	$ _____	÷ 12 =	$ _____
4. AUTOMOBILE	$ _____	÷ 12 =	$ _____
5. ANNUAL INSURANCE	$ _____	÷ 12 =	$ _____
(Life)	($ _____	÷ 12 =	$ _____)
(Medical)	($ _____	÷ 12 =	$ _____)
(Auto)	($ _____	÷ 12 =	$ _____)
(Home)	($ _____	÷ 12 =	$ _____)
6. CLOTHING	$ _____	÷ 12 =	$ _____
7. INVESTMENTS	$ _____	÷ 12 =	$ _____
8. OTHER	$ _____	÷ 12 =	$ _____
	$ _____	÷ 12 =	$ _____

FORM 3

CHAPTER 5

Straight Talk from Larry on Marriage

CHAPTER 5

Straight Talk from Larry on Marriage

Q: *Larry, early in the workbook you speak of finances functioning like a "doorway to intimacy." Why are finances such an important topic for engaged couples?*

LARRY: I believe that finances are simply outward indicators of a person's spiritual condition. You can tell a great deal about the emotional and spiritual maturity of people by the way they handle their finances. People who are sloppy with their finances will have sloppiness show up elsewhere in their habits and attitudes. And the opposite is true: People who are responsible with their money will have responsibility reflected elsewhere in their lives.

The purpose of the engagement period is to literally prepare for marriage by really getting to know one another. Without a specific plan for the engagement, the time can easily degenerate into nothing more than marking days off the calendar until the wedding. Reviewing money management can play a major role in premarital counseling. This material should be considered essential by engaged couples, parents, and pastors alike.

Q: *Larry, credit card debt continues to mushroom in America. Do you recommend that newlyweds avoid credit cards altogether? If not, under what conditions should they use them?*

LARRY: Credit cards are not the problem. It's the *misuse* of credit cards that gets people into trouble. I believe that every credit card should have the following warning on it: DANGER! USE OF THIS CARD CAN BE INJURIOUS TO YOUR MARRIAGE. I don't object to couples using credit cards as a matter of convenience, but I do think they should be used under the following strict rules.

1. A working budget must be a prerequisite to the use of credit cards. Without a budget, there is no meaningful context to determine if a particular purchase can be afforded. So it's simple: No budget, no cards.
2. Both partners should agree to use credit cards only to purchase items provided for in their budget. In other words, unplanned or impulse purchases will lead to trouble.
3. Balances of each credit card should be paid in full at the end of the month, with no exceptions.
4. The first time these rules are violated, the couple should cut up the cards and throw them away.

These rules set up tight boundaries for the use of credit cards. Basically, they can be used as a matter of convenience. If they're used to borrow or impose on the future, that attitude will surely lead to trouble. It's fun to get into debt, but it's painful to pay off those balances. *"The wicked borrows and does not pay back, but the righteous is gracious and gives"* (Psalm 37:21).

Q: *Are there other precautions a couple can take to be sure that a credit card doesn't get out of hand?*

LARRY: One step is to obtain a *secured* bank card. Let's say the bank gives you a Visa or MasterCard with a credit limit of $500. The couple simply needs to deposit $500, or an amount equal to the credit limit, into a savings account at the bank. The money becomes a guarantee that the account will be paid in full each month.

Q: *What advice do you have for the engaged couple who plan to bring substantial debt into the marriage?*

LARRY: If the combined debt payments are going to exceed the percentage outlined in the budget guidelines, I recommend they consider postponing the marriage until progress is made on the debts. And the more debt there is, the more urgent a delay in the marriage becomes. Beginning a marriage with a heavy debt load is like starting a marathon with a broken leg.

It's hard to heal when you constantly keep the problem under stress.

Habitual debt should trigger the couple to candidly address their attitudes about money. We've provided the surveys in this workbook to help bring the key issues into focus, but it's up to the couple to determine the particular financial circumstances they will live with.

If a couple decides to marry in spite of the debt they carry, they should be prepared to make substantial sacrifices in other areas of their budget to allow for the debt repayments. Obviously it's better to start marriage with a clean slate.

Q: *Many couples are eager to establish credit as a new family. How can they do that without getting into major debt?*

LARRY: One way is to obtain a small loan, $500 to $1,000, and use the money to pay installments to the bank. They'll lose a little bit of money on interest but they'll establish a track record with the bank. Also, being on time with rent or mortgage payments will help.

Q: *What are the most common problem areas couples face with their monthly budgeting?*

LARRY: First, there's the challenge of adjusting from the lifestyle of a single to married life. Lifestyles change after marriage, including how often to eat out, what to spend on entertainment, what kind of automobiles to drive, where to live, and what to spend on clothing.

One of the most common problem areas in a new budget is housing. I often see young couples trying to purchase too much house too soon. They become saddled with a huge mortgage payment, and that throws the rest of the budget out of balance.

Another common mistake is going into debt to set up housekeeping. Following the marriage, there's almost a surge to duplicate what their parents or friends have in the way of furniture, appliances, and so forth. The danger is getting saddled with long-term monthly payments that the couple really can't afford. Since it is expensive to set up housekeeping, the couple should make allowance for this when making their wedding plans.

Q: *Speaking of housing, under what conditions should newlyweds consider purchasing their first home?*

LARRY: Some will already own a house when they get married. But for those who don't, here are some factors to consider. First, I would allow up to a year for the couple to settle into a routine with their budget. It will likely take that long to really establish their monthly expenses.

Next, the couple should have a pretty firm idea that they will be living in the same location for at least the next three years. Anything under that, it's probably better to rent while continuing to save toward a down payment. I would not encourage a couple to purchase if they have to take a second mortgage to finance closing costs or the down payment.

Finally, they should be sure that their entire housing expenditures will fit within the monthly budget, not just their house payment. The total housing budget include utilities, maintenance, insurance, and taxes.

Q: *Larry, you've spoken out against prenuptial agreements. Don't they provide a "safety valve" in case the marriage doesn't work out?*

LARRY: Prenuptial agreements are plans to distribute assets in the event a marriage does not work out. I think it's far wiser for the couple to invest time into making the marriage work, rather than planning for the marriage to fail. A marriage must be built on trust. If you can't trust your partner before marriage, how can you trust him or her afterward?

Prenuptial agreements are simply an indication that the couple hasn't grown deep enough in trust and intimacy to be ready for marriage. Those who insist on a prenuptial agreement should postpone the wedding until they are ready to become totally united as a couple.

Q: *What would you say to the couple that intends to marry but plans to keep separate bank accounts?*

LARRY: They are not ready to get married. When God says in Genesis 2:24 that a man and woman become "one flesh," He's not just talking about the physical sense. God created marriage as the highest, most honored, most intimate of all human relationships. As such, the husband-wife relationship takes precedence over blood-kin ties. Now that's remarkable. That means a man is closer to his wife than his own mother from whom he was born, and that a woman is closer to her husband than the children she will bear from her own body. Unwillingness to join all assets and bank accounts after marriage is a danger signal that unresolved trust issues are yet lingering in the relationship.

Q: *Thinking that they have their whole lives ahead of them and that they don't own much, many couples neglect to write a will. What's your advice to them?*

LARRY: I would encourage every couple to prepare a will immediately. True, they may not have much in the way of material assets, but if one partner tragically dies an untimely death, and there is a wrongful death settlement or large insurance settlement, suddenly their estate can be worth quite a lot.

I know death is not pleasant to think about, especially in the context of wedding plans. But the Bible says *"It is appointed for men to die once, and after this comes judgment"* (Hebrews 9:27). Like it or not, everyone lives in mortal bodies and, sooner or later, will depart this life. For some, it's sooner than later, so the wise thing is to be prepared.

Q: *Can a couple really "divorce-proof" their marriage?*

LARRY: I not only think they can, but I believe that's what God expects. While the exact words may differ, most couples plan to exchange wedding vows in which they pledge themselves to one another through better or worse, sickness and health, richer or poorer (basically under all circumstances) until they are parted by death. They also pledge themselves to marital fidelity, meaning their partner will be their only sexual partner for life. Ecclesiastes 5:4–5 says, *"When you make a vow to God, do not be late in paying it, for He takes no delight in fools. Pay what you vow! It is better that you should not vow than that you should vow and not pay."* I would encourage couples to simply throw the word divorce out of their vocabulary and not even consider it as a remote option. And if they're not willing to keep the vows they exchange, they're not ready to get married.

Q: *It's not unusual for parents to want to help the newlyweds get started financially by offering gifts. Is this a good idea?*

LARRY: I encourage parents to share from their resources while they are still living. That way they can see how the money is being spent. But I would caution that these gifts should be limited to special occasions such as the wedding itself, Christmas, birthdays, anniversaries, and so forth.

Ongoing financial support is another issue. Newlyweds should be prepared to take responsibility for their own finances and plan to live within their means. A couple who continually depend on Mom and Dad to bail them out or to provide money for items in a normal budget can eventually drive a wedge in the marriage. The newly married couple should be prepared to cut the financial strings to their parents and stand on their own.

Q: *Larry, some Christians struggle with the issue of life insurance, believing that it is unscriptural and demonstrates a lack of faith in God. What advice do you have for newlyweds on that topic?*

LARRY: That's a tough question. It's true that insurance is not specifically defined in Scripture, but the principle of making future provision is. In fact, the broad concept of insurance is based on a biblical principle from 2 Corinthians 8:14.

The key is having a right motive for obtaining insurance. If someone buys life insurance for protection, I think that's a mistaken attitude. God alone is our protector, and we should properly place our faith in Him. But purchasing insurance for provision in a time of emergency or sudden death is scriptural.

"A prudent man sees evil and hides himself, the naive proceed and pay the penalty" (Proverbs 27:12).

Q: *You recommend that pastors link newlyweds with older couples in the church. Why is that?*

LARRY: Two reasons. First, the new couple will establish their patterns of money management in the first year of marriage. What they do for the first year will be foundational for many years to come. Many problems in the years ahead can be averted with wise counsel for the couple in that first year of marriage.

The second reason is for accountability. Naive or impulsive spending mistakes are less likely for a couple if they know they have someone to periodically check in with. I realize a relationship like this might feel a bit intrusive; but, remember, mismanagement of personal finances is a huge contributing factor to the divorce rate in this country.

Taking this step is one way the church can actively get involved in saving marriages. I believe the biblical principles that support this can be found in 2 Timothy 2:2 and Titus 2:2–8.

Q: *Since the Bible describes the husband as the spiritual leader of the family, shouldn't he be the one to pay the bills?*

LARRY: Not necessarily. Being responsible as the leader doesn't mean he's a dictator; nor does it mean the couple shouldn't discuss and agree on financial management. Both people should be involved in paying the monthly bills. Doing so will keep both partners fully aware of their financial status.

Practically speaking, however, only one person should keep the books. The personality tests in this workbook should highlight which person is more analytical and detail oriented. And even though one person primarily handles balancing the checkbook, both should be fully trained and able to do it. The couple might decide to switch these responsibilities every six months or so.

Q: *Should every expenditure be discussed and agreed upon?*

LARRY: I think the couple should come to an agreement on the amount of money that can be spent without first checking with each other. The specific amount will depend on the budget category and the couple's particular circumstance.

Also, I think the couple should budget a modest amount of personal spending money for miscellaneous needs.

CHAPTER 6

The Pastor's Guide

CHAPTER 6
The Pastor's Guide

This workbook has been created with the knowledge that mismanagement of finances plays a major role in today's high divorce rate. For couples who stay married, personal finances can prove to be a constant source of argument and struggle, unless biblical principles are adopted.

Because you are committed to the well-being of the married couples in your church, I know you share these same concerns. I believe this workbook can help you lead couples in a realistic preparation for marriage.

There are two ways this workbook can be used.

1. I recommend that you give a copy of the workbook to each couple being counseled. They should complete assigned chapters prior to each counseling session. Obviously, the couple should work through the exercises together. There may be surprises along the way as they discover each other's values, attitudes, and motives.

The workbook is designed to help couples evaluate their relationship in general and their attitudes about money in particular. The goal is to help them adopt the biblical attitude of managers or stewards who do just what their masters say to do.

A second goal is to trigger in-depth communication prior to marriage. Complete honesty before marriage sets the tone for the entire marriage. Encourage each couple to make note of unresolved issues they discover and plan to discuss those issues with you.

They should not be made to feel as if they are being "audited." Instead, as their pastor, you're simply showing interest because you care for their future marriage. Be aware, however, that some couples may choose to either postpone or completely cancel their wedding plans as a result of utilizing these materials.

If you have a number of weddings and cannot personally review the progress of each couple, perhaps you can pair them with an associate on your staff or with a mature, business-wise couple in the church. The new couple likely will benefit from some accountability to these contacts in the months *after* marriage.

2. A second use of the workbook could be as an outreach in your community. Knowing that many weddings take place in the months of June through August, you might offer a class for engaged couples during the preceding January. This could prove to be an effective outreach tool for this group and help to cement a relationship between them and your church.

To teach such a class, simply use the workbook to offer general observations on the chapter topics, combined with other materials you typically teach in premarital counseling. In other words, say to an entire group what you would say to a couple. You may want to prepare by using some of the materials listed at the close of this section. In addition, your presentations could be followed by group exercises and discussion. Of course, you would not want to deal with any one couple's specific situation in a group setting.

The workbook follows a logical flow:

- introduction to the concepts of money being a "doorway to intimacy" and biblical stewardship
- understanding one's personality strengths and weaknesses and how to work as a team
- discovering one's tendencies of financial management
- charting current financial obligations
- preparing the first budget
- answering common questions from newlyweds.

To become totally familiar with the workbook, I would encourage you and your wife to work through it together.

To further assist you in the premarital counseling process, I have listed several resources below.

Two Masters (52-minute video)
The Complete Financial Guide for Young Couples (Victor Press)
Debt-Free Living (Moody Press)
Using Your Money Wisely (Moody Press)
Your Finances in Changing Times (Moody Press)
How to Manage Your Money (Moody Press)

If you are not familiar with the DISC model of personality used in Chapter 2, the resources below contain a more in-depth discussion. Both books are available through Christian Financial Concepts.

Your Career in Changing Times by Larry Burkett and Lee Ellis (Moody Press)
Understanding How Others Mis-Understand You by Ken Voges and Ron Braund
    (Moody Press)

Another resource to be aware of: the 1,000 CFC-trained financial counselors across the country, who may be contacted for additional help.

For the counselor nearest you, address your request to:

    Counseling Department
    Christian Financial Concepts
    PO Box 2377
    Gainesville, GA 30503-2377

DISC Word Definitions

(Definitions to be used with the Couples Communication Survey in Chapter 2)

Row 1—

    Enthusiastic: high energy, eagerness, and zeal
    Loyal: faithful and dependable
    Detailed: careful attention to the particular
    Commanding: directs others with authority

Row 2—

    Lenient: not strict
    Expressive: easily communicates thoughts and feelings
    Decisive: capable of making decisions or solving problems
    Particular: attentive to details

Row 3—

    Convincing: ability to be persuasive
    Tough-Minded: determined, not easily swayed
    Meticulous: extremely careful and precise
    Kind: friendly, generous, and warmhearted

Row 4—

    Independent: self-reliant, free from control of others
    Follow rules: preference for following established procedures
    Peaceful: calm, free from hostility or quarrels
    Fun-Loving: playful, enjoys pleasure, jokes, amusement

Row 5—

    High standards: insists on high quality or precision
    Understanding: capable of discerning the thoughts or feelings of others

People-Oriented: prefers to interact with people
Daring: willing to take risks, adventurous

Row 6—

Charitable: generously gives to the needs of others
Lively: energetic, vigorous, full of life
Risk Taker: daring; willing to take chances
Serious: concerned with important matters

Row 7—

Cheerful: happy, pleasant, and willing in disposition
Courageous: faces danger with confidence, brave
Precise: exact, definite, distinct, or correct
Merciful: full of compassion

Row 8—

Confident: full of assurance and certainty
Logical: able to reason clearly
Supportive: furnishes assistance with practical needs
Inspiring: stimulates the mind or emotions of others

Row 9—

Conscientious: thorough, painstakingly careful
Patient: capable of calmly enduring, tolerant
Good Mixer: sociable, interacts with people easily
Fearless: bold, unafraid, brave

Row 10—

Non-conforming: resists rules, bounds, or customs of others
Talkative: inclined to talk frequently
Gentle: kind, friendly or patient
Analytical: given to careful, methodical examination

Row 11—

Organized: orderly, systematic, or arranged
Assertive: states one's position boldly
Popular: widely liked and appreciated
Even-Paced: steady and consistent

Row 12—

Good Listener: pays careful attention to what is said
Factual: based on facts rather than rumor or innuendo
Take-Charge: assumes responsibility or command
Uninhibited: open, free from traditional constraints

Row 13—

Aggressive: bold or assertive
Cooperative: capable of working together
Vibrant: high energy or activity
Accurate: free from errors, correct

Row 14—

Efficient: works with a minimum of waste
Direct: candid, frank, or straightforward
Gracious: kind, courteous, compassionate, merciful
Excitable: capable of being easily excited

Row 15—

Influencing: causes others to change their minds or course of action
Accommodating: responsive or helpful to others
Focused: concentrated interest, not distracted
Frank: candid, straightforward, direct, open

Row 16—

Agreeable: pleasant and pleasing to others
Animated: lively, vigorous, energetic
Forceful: pushy, direct, persuasive
Systematic: methodical and purposeful

Larry Burkett, founder and president of Christian Financial Concepts, is the best-selling author of 47 books on business and personal finances and two novels. He also hosts two radio programs broadcast on hundreds of stations worldwide.

Larry holds degrees in marketing and finance, and for several years served as a manager in the space program at Cape Canaveral, Florida. He also has been vice president of an electronics manufacturing firm. Larry's education, business experience, and solid understanding of God's Word enable him to give practical, Bible-based financial counsel to families, churches, and businesses.

Founded in 1976, Christian Financial Concepts is a nonprofit, nondenominational ministry dedicated to helping God's people gain a clear understanding of how to manage their money according to scriptural principles. Although practical assistance is provided on many levels, the purpose of CFC is simply to bring glory to God by freeing His people from financial bondage so they may serve Him to their utmost.

One major avenue of ministry involves the training of volunteers in budget and debt counseling and linking them with financially troubled families and individuals through a nationwide referral network. CFC also provides financial management seminars and workshops for churches and other groups. (Formats available include audio, video, and live instruction.) A full line of printed and audio-visual materials related to money management is available through CFC's materials department (1-800-722-1976).

Career Pathways, another outreach of Christian Financial Concepts, helps teenagers and adults find their occupational calling. The Career Pathways "Assessment" gauges a person's work priorities, skills, vocational interests, and personality. Reports in each of these areas define a person's strengths, weaknesses, and unique, God-given pattern for work.

For further information about the ministry of Christian Financial Concepts, write to:

Christian Financial Concepts
PO Box 2458
Gainesville, Georgia 30503-2458

OTHER BOOKS BY LARRY BURKETT
Available at your local bookstore

The Financial Planning Workbook

This workbook includes practical advice about managing your finances and provides a series of easy-to-follow worksheets that allow you to structure and maintain your family's budget. Larry shows you where to start, how to stay on track, and even addresses special budgeting problems. Extra worksheets are included.

The Word on Finances

This useful tool contains a collection of relevant Scriptures arranged under eight comprehensive headings. Larry's practical wisdom opens each of the more than seventy topical selections.

Debt-Free Living

This book is for anyone whose money ran out before the month did. Again. Or even if your financial situation hasn't reached a crisis point, you will benefit from Larry's wise counsel. Through case studies of several marriages helped through proper financial counsel, Larry shows how to become and remain debt-free. He warns about the kinds of credit to avoid and provides specific how-to's for solving debt problems. *Debt-Free Living* remains a best-seller, with more than 150,000 copies in print.

How to Manage Your Money

There is so much religious "folklore" regarding money that few Christians understand God's true will in finances. But the Scriptures have plenty to say about how we should handle the funds entrusted to us. There are more than 700 direct references to money in the Bible and hundreds more indirect references. *How to Manage Your Money*, a Bible study by Larry Burkett, brings many of these references to light as it introduces Christians to the "scriptural" view of finances. This workbook covers such topics as stewardship, short- and long-range planning, tithing, and much more.

Your Finances in Changing Times

With more than a million copies in print, this book is a perfect introduction to basic financial management. It is a complete money guide, offering biblical concepts and practical suggestions for building a sound financial program. Learn to plan for the future, get out or stay out of debt, and much more.

Moody Press, a ministry of Moody Bible Institute,
is designed for education, evangelization, and edification.
If we may assist you in knowing more about Christ
and the Christian life, please write us without obligation:
Moody Press, c/o MLM, Chicago, Illinois 60610.